Congregations and Pastors

Reflections on the Work of the Church

by John A. Esau

Faith & Life Press
Newton, Kansas
Winnipeg, Manitoba

Herald
Press

Herald Press
Scottdale, Pennsylvania
Waterloo, Ontario

Printed in the United States of America.

Library of Congress Catalog Card Number 99-72565

International Standard Book Number 0-87303-348-5

Cover design by Philip Sawatzky; back cover photo by Vada Snider; book layout by Ilene Franz; printing by Mennonite Press.

"John Esau certainly succeeded in his goal to write for lay leaders as well as pastors. John encourages frank discussion on hard topics such as the pastor's salary, anonymous letters, the role of ushers, and church secretaries. His words are always heartfelt, full of truth, and measured with grace." —Anne Stuckey, minister of congregational leadership, Mennonite Church

"These are marvelous nuggets. This collection of articles offer a rich feast of insights on how to do ministry in an effective and mature fashion. John Esau is a wise counselor, and his wisdom provides intelligent and creative guidance to both clergy and laity." —Wilson Yeats, president, United Theological Seminary of the Twin Cities

"The ideas, insights, and suggestions offered here are crucial for productive ministry, healthy congregations, and mutually supportive relationships between pastors and congregations. It is written for lay readership in non-academic and non-technical language." —Marvin H. Ewert, lay leader, Newton, Kansas

"A bountiful harvest of insight and wise counsel from a lifetime of ministry. This book is full of common sense commentary on church life that will instruct, delight, and challenge pastors and congregations alike." —Nelson Kraybill, president, Associated Mennonite Biblical Seminary

"John captures our imagination with provocative phrases and questions. Then he offers alternative perspectives that turn problems upside down and suggest new opportunities. His insights are practical, pointed, and deeply spiritual. I think every new pastor should receive this book as a 'Welcome to Ministry' gift." —Fred Unruh, pastor, Lethbridge, Alberta

Contents

Foreword

The headline on John Esau's first column in *Mennonite Weekly Review* was "You Can Help Make Your Church Better." That sums up why his "Congregations and Pastors" is *MWR*'s most popular column.

The headline from the April 1988 issue assumes two things: There's room for improvement, and you can make a difference. When people care deeply about a writer's subject—as Esau's readers care about the church—that's a winning combination.

It's a combination that arises from Esau's way of thinking. He's an optimist. He writes with a hopeful attitude because he believes God has given us the ability to make the church fulfill its mission better. Sometimes all we need to get started is a fresh idea from a person whose knowledge comes from experience. Through his column, Esau has been that person.

"Congregations and Pastors" links three elements that make good columns: They're informative, interesting, and useful. They're informative because they offer glimpses into how other congregations and other people do things. Columns such as "Preaching: Inspiration, Hard Work," help church members understand the challenges a pastor faces. Other columns show us how different congregations organize their ministries, set policies, and follow traditions. We often see ourselves in the situations Esau describes.

One reason the columns are interesting is that they're thought-provoking. The last column in this collection, "Belief, Unbelief Both Take Faith," offers clear insight on how believers and unbelievers both live in tension between faith and uncertainty. Some columns are interesting in the human-interest sense, like "My Father, the Blind Evangelist."

They're useful by giving practical advice. This ranges from broad themes, such as "Seek First to Understand Others," to details such as "Asking Correctly to Get Volunteers." Readers also enjoy Esau's uncommon common sense in columns like "Say It Again So They Won't Forget," "A Church Is Not a Museum," and "You Can't Clone Your Old Pastor."

Perhaps no institution touches on so many aspects of life— spirituality, education, administration, interpersonal relationships, finance, helping those in need—as does the church. Esau fulfills the ambitious goal of giving good advice on just about everything congregations do.

Readers will quickly sense that Esau writes because he loves the church. He expresses that motive most directly in the column "Why I Believe in the Church." He says: "In the church I have found, as nowhere else, a genuine and honest quest to make sense of life in all its dimensions. I believe in the church because it has given me meaning and hope."

The New Testament epistles often mention the importance of encouraging each other in the faith. Esau's writings place him among the leading encouragers of the church today.

Paul Schrag
Editor, Mennonite Weekly Review
January 30, 1999

Introduction

As a pastor, I regularly subscribed to and read journals dealing with pastoral ministry and the life and work of our congregations. These were helpful to me, but I often wondered how these important but practical issues might be shared with others in the congregation. I often thought these ideas about congregational life and pastoral ministry were directed to a too limited audience.

With that in mind, I finally drew up a proposal for a regular column to be entitled simply: "Congregations and Pastors." I intentionally chose the newspaper format of the *Mennonite Weekly Review*, which had a broad readership of conference leaders, pastors, and laity within our faith tradition. I wanted it to appear often enough that there would be a sense of continuity and an anticipation of things to come. I also wanted the columns to be short enough that they would be read when a new issue arrived rather than laid aside for future reading, then forgotten.

Above all, I hoped to have members of our congregations as the primary readers, so the language and style needed to remain popular. This was not a column for scholars or even primarily for pastors, but for the average member of the church. It was directed to those who loved the church and desired to see it become the loving, faithful community of believers God intends.

This column, therefore, had its origin in a pastor's desire to increase the dialogue among all Christians about how we live out our relationships in the community we call the church. I am glad for the pastors who have been readers. But I have been even more gratified by the responses I have received from other members of our congregations. In a real sense the column has been directed toward lay leaders in our congregations, and it is they who have been most generous and affirming throughout these eleven years.

I have taken special delight in the occasional "complaint" of pastors who have felt compelled to read the column because their members were talking about it!

Most of us, pastors and laity alike, live with two conflicting feelings about the church. We know that it can be something very good, the means by which God offers us life and faith in Christ, the opportunity to discover meaningful relationships with other people, a place to grow, and a channel through which to give ourselves in service and mission. That is the ideal.

Sometimes the reality we experience is otherwise, and the church becomes for us a place of pain, disappointment, and occasionally even disillusionment. Many people realize that all is not well with the church, but we are offered little guidance to do anything about it. So we blame the problems on someone—most often, on the pastor.

There are books that hold grand visions for the church, ways in which we can think boldly as we move into the third Christian millennium. This is not one of those books. Its goals are more modest, though not less ideal. It asks for small, incremental ways we can live out our faith in the church community.

There are ways we can make a difference by helping to establish healthy congregations and positive, effective pastor-congregation relationships. There are better ways pastors can live out their unique and necessary role as the spiritual teachers, leaders, and mentors of our congregations.

I have addressed issues dealing with pastoral ministry. How do pastors manage their time effectively, and how can the congregation respect the need for pastors to have privacy and time off? What about ministerial ethics? What factors lead to success and failure in ministry? The list goes on and on.

There is a comparably long list of issues related to congregational life. How do we go about finding good leadership in our churches? When should the church call in the conference minister for help? How can we create a more positive reporting system of our financial stewardship? Are large churches good or bad? What are good options and poor options for handicapped accessibility? Again the potential would appear to be endless.

I don't pretend to have all the answers. What I do hope is that the column, and now this book, will provide sufficient "grist for the mill" so that pastors and members of our congregations will be stimulated to discuss and sometimes debate important issues. The goal is to help us activate our faith in living, growing congregations. It is, after all, in our congregations where "the rubber hits the road"; and it is there where faith becomes action.

When I began to look over the work of eleven years of writing, I quickly discerned that what I had written represented the two streams of Christian faith that continue to shape my life and ministry. I am a child of the Mennonite/Anabaptist faith heritage, and I claim that faith as my own. I have worked specifically in the General Conference family of Mennonite churches. But I also know myself as an ecumenical Christian whose faith embraces and cares about the larger Christian heritage and community.

About half of what I have written was directed toward the unique aspects of Mennonite congregations. The other half addressed a broader Christian perspective and was not burdened by references to things Mennonite. This book is the collection of the latter. It intends to invite Christians of many traditions to consider the universal issues of our life together.

I wrote my first column in March 1988, on an old portable Smith Corona typewriter which my parents had purchased somewhere about 1940. That typewriter remains on its old typing table in my office as a symbol of my links to the past and to those who have come before me. To them I owe a great debt of gratitude, especially to my father John J. Esau who, despite his 50-plus years of blindness, was a faithful servant of Christ and the church.

3

Writers of public documents know how much they are indebted to the work of others. Shelley Buller, administrative assistant in the General Board office of the General Conference Mennonite Church, retyped many of the earlier columns and has been a supporting colleague throughout. My thanks to Robert Schrag, publisher of *Mennonite Weekly Review*, who saw potential in the original proposal for this column and invited me to begin writing. Paul Schrag, editor of *Mennonite Weekly Review*, did the essential editorial work which always improved what had been submitted.

Bernice, my companion in life and in ministry, has been a faithful supporter in these extra endeavors of work. Her intuitive sense of theology, her care about the church, and her occasional critique have been valuable assets. My special thanks is reserved for her in all that she has been as a spouse and as a kindred spirit in the journey of faith.

From a typewriter to a computer, the means used in writing this column symbolizes the changes that are affecting our changing world and the nature of how pastors work with words. But what has not changed is the quality of the relationships that must exist between pastors and congregations if their common witness to the gospel of Christ is to make a difference in our world.

John A. Esau
Newton, Kansas
December 15, 1998

1. How Many Volunteers Do You Have?

I am amazed that we have as many people as we do giving of their time to energize the working of our congregations.

One of the regular complaints one hears in church circles these days is that too few people are willing to volunteer their time for the ministries of the church. Having heard that one too many times, I decided to count how many volunteer tasks were regularly being filled in our congregation.

The result was surprising! In a congregation of 500 participating people, I came up with a list of about 600 active volunteer roles that people were carrying out. This is in a congregation where the majority of adults are employed and a high percentage of people work more than full time in their professions. How did I arrive at such a number? Let me trace the process so that you can develop comparable figures for your congregation.

First of all, this is what I did not count. I did not count the dozens of people who bake pies and do other things for relief sales. I did not count the numerous people who make Jell-O salads and bake cakes for funerals. and other events in the church and community. I did not count Sunday morning greeters who take their annual turn, nor did I count people who show up for spring and fall church cleaning. I did not count the volunteer help given to local church institutions.

So what went into those 600 volunteer tasks? I began by asking myself which tasks in the church are sustained over a period of time, and require repeated and regular involvement. I began by listing everyone who serves on church boards, commissions, and committees. Next I counted the ushers, and since we have four different groups, that turned out to be a substantial number.

Then I listed those who give their time and energy to teaching Sunday school classes, including other classes during the week. The women's fellowship involves many women in leadership roles, and more recently the men have reorganized, although with simpler leadership.

What about music? We often forget that people who sing in choirs volunteer their time for rehearsal during the week, so I counted all the choir members, including youth and children. They count too, don't they? And in most of our churches we would add the choir directors, organists, and pianists as volunteers.

Others give time to leadership for junior and senior high youth. And some churches have regular volunteer visitation teams, and other churches have . . .

The point is that we have many, many more volunteers working than most of us realize. We ought to be grateful rather than complain. I am amazed that we have as many people as we do giving of their time to energize the working of our congregations.

I also learned that the proportion of volunteers to church membership was about the same in a large congregation as in a small congregation. A reasonable goal might well be one volunteer task for every active member, regardless of the size of the church.

I often hear churches suggest that they don't want to hire additional pastoral staff because they want their members to become more involved in volunteering to meet the needs of the congregation. In large congregations with 250 members or more, that never works. It takes more pastoral staff rather than less to have a large volunteer network active in a congregation.

June 2, 1988

2. Pastors Must Be Good Administrators

Good pastoral administration is the oil that reduces the friction so that the complex parts can work together.

When I began my years of ministry, I brought into it certain ideals about what a minister should and should not do. Somewhere in my seminary training I picked up the notion that one thing the pastor should not do is the administration work needed in a congregation. "Leave administration to lay people who, after all, can do it better anyhow," seemed to be the line we heard and believed.

I no longer believe that. In fact, I think one cannot successfully pastor a congregation without both some commitment to and skill in administration. The administrative role of the pastor is still the most undervalued ingredient in pastoral leadership.

It is common to believe that the leadership ability of a pastor is best seen and best tested in the public roles of preaching and teaching. A person who brings skill and energy, or "charisma," is perceived as a leader. To the contrary, I think the best test of leadership is not in those public roles but in the long-term effective administrative abilities of pastors.

Ardean Goertzen, in his research project on pastoral leadership, heard this message loud and clear from church members. Many people complained that pastors were not sufficiently committed to doing "something practical about church administration."

This complaint was mentioned more often about pastors who were in the process of leaving the ministry. That only proves my point: To be successful in ministry one must exercise the gift of administration.

Several metaphors describe part of the task of administration. We speak about the glue that holds a church together; good

7

administration keeps a congregation from flying in all directions at once.

My pastor recently told me about his moment of insight when he realized that, as pastor, he knew more than anyone else about the congregation, its members and its program. The responsible use of that information can serve as administrative glue to keep a congregation functioning effectively.

The second metaphor related to pastoral administration is oil. As a young pastor the one thing I did not want to do was "oil the machinery of the church" to keep it running smoothly. I now know that this is an essential part of good pastoral administration. A church, as any human group, produces friction when it is active and working. Good pastoral administration is the oil that reduces the friction so that the complex parts can work together.

Another aspect of administration in the church is one for which I don't have a metaphor, but it has to do with planning. It is the task of looking toward the future and helping the congregation initiate new programs and activities and set new goals.

Here, of course, is where leadership is tested. Pastors need to remember that the right to exercise this kind of leadership is only granted to those who have first proven their responsible administrative gifts as glue and oil!

June 16, 1988

3. Involving Members As Worship Leaders

Pastors are really doing their job and doing it effectively when they don't do everything themselves.

Pastors are often caught between a rock and a hard place. Take, for instance, the question of whether lay members of the congregation should participate in leading worship on Sunday morning.

If pastors involve members of their congregations in leading the call to worship, reading the Scripture, and leading in the morning prayer, they are accused of being lazy and not doing their job. If, on the other hand, pastors never invite congregational members to share in worship leadership, they run the risk of being accused of controlling everything and not allowing others to participate with their gifts.

It's an argument on which I wouldn't waste any time or energy. Everyone benefits when members of the congregation participate in active worship leadership.

Does it save the pastor time? Absolutely not. It takes far more time to help members prepare for this responsibility than it would to do it oneself. Does it make it easier for the pastor? No, again. It takes far more emotional energy wondering if things will go as smoothly and correctly as they would if the pastor had complete control.

Does involving members in worship leadership have any benefits? Definitely yes. Its greatest benefit comes to the people involved. It causes them to become more aware of how a worship service is put together and needs to flow together.

It gives them an increased sense of participation when they see their Christian brothers and sisters leading on other Sundays. It increases their sense of self-worth and gives them the opportunity to know that they can make an important spiritual contribution to the life of the congregation.

It also offers benefits to the church. Try as one will, it is impossible for the pastor to come up with a fresh and new prayer for the congregation every Sunday. Our congregation has been greatly enriched by the prayers of lay members, many of whom have given careful thought and preparation to this important spiritual moment.

Leading in public worship is not for everyone, and I would never force anyone into it. But many more people can and should be invited to participate. Some young people might receive their first experience in church leadership in this way and thus, begin to hear the call to ministry.

In our congregation some of us will never forget the Sunday that the worship service was led by Elliot Regier, who lives with Down's syndrome. Harold Peters, limited to a wheelchair by his severe arthritis, led worship on another Sunday.

I especially remember one mother's prayer given during Advent as she was preparing for Christmas. I recall a teacher's prayer shared when a comet neared the earth during another Advent. These were high spiritual moments, led by members of our congregation.

It does not need to happen every Sunday. On plenty of Sundays it will be most appropriate for the pastor to lead in the morning prayer. But let no one criticize pastors on Sundays when they invite members of the congregation to share in leading worship. Pastors are really doing their job and doing it effectively when they don't do everything themselves.

July 21, 1988

4. Former Pastors Must Learn to Say "No"

A former pastor returning to provide ministerial functions does more than hurt the ego of the present pastor.

I just got off the phone with one of our pastors who is undergoing considerable pain in relation to some members in the congregation. It was a story all too familiar.

A few members are voicing strong dissent against the pastoral leadership. "He is not providing spiritual leadership. His spouse is too busy pursuing her interests and not fulfilling her volunteer role as the pastor's wife. Their children (junior high age) dress too much like their peers!"

The former pastor was dearly loved and able to get along with everyone. In fact, he recently went back to perform a wedding in the church with a family of the dissenting group. He had checked with the current pastor, of course, and was told it was all right to proceed.

Well, what else could the present pastor say? The fact is that it wasn't all right. It only helped to confirm in the minds of the dissenters that the present pastor was quite dispensable. As far as they were concerned, he wasn't their pastor.

I have identified two issues: (1) the pain which many, if not most, pastors feel from vigorous dissent toward their ministry at some time or another, and (2) the particular problem of former pastors returning to carry out ministry functions in their former congregations. Let me address only the latter.

I have been told by several pastors of situations where former pastors have returned to their congregations to carry out ministry functions: funerals, weddings, and pastoral visitations. In every case, it was a source of considerable pain to the current pastor, who felt caught in a situation where he had no good options.

A former pastor returning to provide ministerial functions does more than hurt the ego of the present pastor. It is an action that is harmful to the life of that congregation. It feeds dissent. It undermines ministry. It generates ill will on the part of the people served. And ultimately it harms the reputation of the former pastor.

There are two solutions to this problem, and both of them are relatively easy. If you are a member of a congregation, don't ask or even consider asking a former pastor to provide a service for your family. If everyone followed this, there would no longer be a problem.

However, if you as a former pastor are asked to return to provide a ministry service for members in a former congregation, you can take the high road and say "no."

Say it gently but firmly. Voice your support for the present pastor, and if you can't do that with integrity, voice your support for the importance of the principle involved.

It is an issue of pastoral ethics. I know that love for people with whom one has felt close kinship in the past pulls at the heartstrings. It is not easy to say no.

But for the sake of the church and the witness for Christ, and ultimately for the welfare of everyone involved, it is essential that former pastors learn to say "no."

August 4, 1988

5. Pastoral Salary Guidelines

The salary a church offers its pastor reflects not only what you think of your pastor but also what you think of your church.

The time for salary review is often an occasion for extra stress in the relationship between pastor and congregation. Because of its complexity, it is easy for each side to use numbers in a way that reflects their biases and expectations. Often communication is at a minimum.

To help ease that process, I am suggesting 10 expectations which pastors can rightfully have of their congregations.

1. That the salary will be reviewed and adjusted annually. This has become an accepted standard procedure, but occasionally I still hear of churches that think a three-year arrangement with the pastor means the salary will remain fixed for the three-year term.

2. That the cost of living adjustment will be the normal minimum increase. Without this minimum adjustment, you are actually asking the pastor to take a salary cut.

3. That there will be some discussion with the pastor during the salary review. My experience is that a good process is as important to the pastor as a good final agreement. The pastor should have some opportunity to share perspectives and expectations. At the minimum the church should expect and even request the pastor to pass on to them any current information regarding salaries which may come to the pastor's attention.

4. That salary guidelines from denominational and area conferences will be taken seriously, even when not followed legalistically. These guidelines have been prepared with careful and responsible thought about current expectations. In some congregations they will be seen as too high, in others as too low. From these guidelines it might be possible to give or take $2,000 to

come up with a reasonable salary range within which congregational discretion will need to be exercised.

5. That appropriate information and comparative data will be gathered for comparable positions in your community. Sometimes it might be helpful to compare with pastors of other denominations. A comparison often made is with people in public education, though this can be tricky. Teachers are often employed for nine or 10 months only, and educational expectations are often less than for pastors. My observation is that school administrators today have moved beyond the range of pastors' salaries, so that is no longer a helpful comparison.

6. That reimbursements will not be included in salary and benefits. Reimbursements such as the mileage allowance based upon miles driven by the pastor in behalf of the church are church expenses not unlike paying the electric bill. I recently learned of one congregation that insisted on treating the mileage allowance as salary and insisted that the minister had to pay income tax on that amount!

7. That churches will provide either in the church budget or in the written agreement adequate distinctions in housing allowance, utilities, and home furnishings so as to minimize the pastor's legal and legitimate tax liability. There is a notion abroad that pastors benefit from special tax breaks. While that is partially true, it is really only a trade-off since the pastor must pay much more social security tax than the average employee.

8. That churches which cannot provide a full-time salary will allow the pastor to seek other part-time employment. It is unfair to say that the church cannot afford a full-time salary yet expect the pastor to work full time, which is normally a minimum of 50 hours a week.

9. That pastors be provided a pension or retirement benefit, usually a sum of 10 percent of base compensation or the cash salary plus housing allowance. Few pastors are independently wealthy even in a modest sense of that word. Without specific provision for retirement income through the working years, pastors will often face very bleak prospects in retirement.

10. That positive, affirming attitudes will guide the entire process. The salary a church offers its pastor reflects not only what you think of your pastor but also what you think of your church.

September 1, 1988

6. Pastors Should Be Teachers, Too

If Christian ministry should find its primary model in Jesus, as I believe it should, then we ought to ask whether the teaching role should be a more central focus of the pastor's responsibility.

Many things are expected of the pastor in the life of the congregation. Some would say we already expect too much. Well, let me add one more role expectation.

I believe that one of the roles for which pastors are best prepared is to serve as a teacher of Scripture, theology, church history and many other areas of learning which are important to the life and growth of all members in a congregation.

This was confirmed recently in a conversation with Perry Yoder, associate professor of Old Testament at Associated Mennonite Biblical Seminary, Elkhart, Ind. I met Yoder following a Sunday morning worship service, and we began talking about the fact that churches seldom think of the pastor as a potential teacher.

Yet consider the fact that, in many congregations, the pastor is the person with the most training and knowledge about how to study the Bible and other areas of religious significance.

Jesus was best known by others as Rabbi, meaning teacher. If Christian ministry should find its primary model in Jesus, as I believe it should, then we ought to ask whether the teaching role should be a more central focus of the pastor's responsibility.

Of course, most pastors are already engaged in some forms of teaching. Most teach the catechism class to youth. Though it is cast in a different form, preaching almost always includes elements of teaching. Some pastors teach mid-week Bible studies. So why ask for anything more?

Many Christians say that formal education has dramatically shaped and revitalized their understanding of faith. It has opened doors to Scripture, broadened their outlook on issues, and helped them become more thoughtful and more committed Christians. Why can't that happen in the church with the pastor as the teacher?

One of the primary contributions pastors can make is to teach not just about the Bible but skills for biblical study. Why should the inductive method of Bible study be the exclusive right of those who have been to seminary? Wouldn't the best contribution pastors might make to their congregations be to help members gain skills to study the Bible for themselves?

Let me suggest an analogy. In Christian social service we have long said it is more important to offer people the ability to produce food for themselves than to offer them free food, except in emergency situations.

In something of the same manner it is far more important to teach our members how to study the Bible for themselves than to offer them the insights which have come to us out of our own Bible study.

I remember Palmer Becker used to talk about the pastor offering the congregation the equivalent of a seminary education over a period of 10 years. It was a noble goal, perhaps too ideal, but it was headed in the right direction.

Perry Yoder related an incident in which he observed the pastor who went to his office and stayed there during the Sunday school hour. "What a wasted resource!" said Yoder. "Why don't churches think of the pastor as a teacher?"

September 15, 1988

7. What Do You Say to the Pastor at the Door?

Do pastors really expect you to say something nice about the sermon every Sunday?

Our coffee conversation this morning began with a story growing out of the weekend. One of our denominational staff persons gave the sermon yesterday in a local congregation.

As is the normal custom, the preacher of the morning was asked to greet the congregation as they departed. One member approached her, exchanged greetings, shook hands, and then said, "That was a nice . . . (brief pause) handshake!"

Stories abound among pastors about the experience they have of greeting the congregation at the end of worship. Handshakes themselves vary from the "limp dishrag" to the "pump handle" to the "vise grip." Recently I shook hands with a woman who nearly took my little finger off, or at least it felt that way.

What do you say to the pastor at the door? Do pastors really expect you to say something nice about the sermon every Sunday? Why do pastors make a weekly ritual of this greeting?

My experience as a pastor is that the stereotyped comment from parishioners, "That was a good sermon, pastor," is almost non-existent. People who do make occasional responses do so sincerely and honestly, because on that particular Sunday the sermon touched a responsive chord.

In other words, the relatively few people who do respond to the sermon are giving genuine affirmations of appreciation, which call for a clear and simple "thank you" from the pastor.

In the early years of my ministry, I felt that this little pastoral ritual was really quite artificial and meaningless. "Why am I doing this?" I asked myself.

Nevertheless, I persisted. Over time I came to discover that important exchanges were happening, even if not on a verbal level of communication. Three important reasons emerged why this ritual is more than a routine.

First, it shows that the pastor is approachable and personal. A fleeting moment of looking into the eyes and face of each other does communicate a bond of caring and an openness to greater exchange if and when the need should arise.

It is a brief encounter of human touch, often without more than "Good morning," in which real grace is nevertheless made personal for both member and pastor. It is also an opportunity to greet the children of the congregation and help them to feel accepted and included.

Second, occasional encounters center on specific personal needs, which members bring to the pastor and in which the ritual of greeting at the door provides the simple opportunity for sharing. I learned that there were times when I stopped to give my full attention to one person for a moment while others went by unnoticed and ungreeted. And they understood.

Third, being available to greet people at the close of worship provided me as the pastor the opportunity to make a first contact with people new to our congregation and to meet other visitors that Sunday. I hope that others in the congregation also take the initiative to welcome these people, so that it is not exclusively the pastor's job. But I found this contact to be valuable.

There were Sundays when the circumstances did not make it natural or easy, and the pastor did not greet people as they departed. We were not legalistic about it, and no one felt called to be critical for that occasional omission.

Better yet, I would on some Sundays try to surprise people by going to the balcony and meeting that part of the congregation. One Easter Sunday, my pastoral colleague and I greeted the congregation as they arrived, which added for all of us a touch of joy and anticipation to the good news of resurrection.

What do you say to the pastor at the door? You don't have to say anything. Above all, be honest. I learned that people respond more to topical sermons than to what I considered more biblical sermons.

I learned to receive the occasional gentle rebuke graciously, and I learned not to act too surprised when someone said something like: "That was a nice . . . handshake."

October 20, 1988

8. Asking Correctly to Get Volunteers

Begin positively and believe that the person being asked will respond positively!

We are almost at the beginning of a new year, and in many congregations that will be a time to identify and call forth new volunteers to serve in the various boards and committees of our congregations.

That sounds like a simple task until you've been in the position of asking others. If you think the responsibility is either simple or easy, you're probably the wrong person to be doing it.

I remember one experience in our church. There was a fairly significant leadership role to be filled. There was no particular crisis in the organization at the time. The church had many capable and competent people who might have carried out the task with joy and even enthusiasm. What happened?

One person accepted the responsibility of finding someone to volunteer for that office. Disaster ensued. Contact after contact was made, each one resulting in a negative response. Ten, 20, and finally 30 people were contacted, and each responded in the same way: "No."

Imagine the consequences. A discouraged volunteer who did the calling. A growing feeling that there is no commitment in the church. The organization for which leadership was being sought was put into a crisis.

What went wrong? When it was too late we learned how the person who volunteered for the task of finding a willing leader went about asking each person. It went something like this: "I have a very difficult job which no one seems to want to do. I'm sure you wouldn't want to be the leader of _____ either, would you?"

What might be learned from such an experience? What are the factors that need to be considered when asking someone else to carry out a responsibility in the church?

1. The most obvious learning from the above experience is not to offer a negative answer for the person you are asking. In the illustration, people were being invited to decline, and to have responded in a positive way would have been awkward and presumptuous. Begin positively and believe that the person being asked will respond positively!

2. If it is indeed a difficult task for which you are asking someone to volunteer, it is appropriate to acknowledge so. To

claim that it would be easy would be misleading and dishonest. But having identified the difficulty of the task, you must go on to state clearly why you believe the person you are asking is capable and should respond as a willing volunteer.

3. Never ask people at random for important jobs. We hear a lot about gift discernment in the church, and we should hear more about what it means. If a short list of potential candidates say "no," then a group needs to come together to plan what to do next. Asking 20, 30, or even 10 candidates in a row without further consultation is never appropriate.

4. Plan for how you ask in line with the level of responsibility of the position. The telephone is entirely appropriate for communication and asking for many minor tasks that need to be done. But don't use the telephone if you are asking someone to give major leadership to a significant responsibility. Face-to-face encounter with the prospective candidate is then essential.

5. Be clear in what you are asking of the person. What is the nature of the job to be done? How much time will it take? How long will the responsibility last? Who else will be involved and supportive? What assistance will be available?

6. While giving a clear call and a challenge to assume responsibility, be careful not to load your invitation with guilt should the person finally say "no." People who feel coerced into something seldom perform the responsibility well. And if they respond because they have been made to feel guilty otherwise, you can be assured of their long-term resentment. Accept an honest and firm "no."

7. Finally, the most sensitive question to consider is: Who is doing the asking? Are they perceived by others as capable and respected? Do they understand themselves what it is that they are asking others to do? How would you respond if they asked you to do something for the church and the kingdom of Christ?

December 15, 1988

9. Learning Members' Time, Talents

The time and talent survey offers the promise of new life, new commitments, new involvement, new energy for a congregation.

One of the popular methods for congregations to work at gift discernment has been through the time and talent surveys of members.

In such a survey members are invited to indicate on a form what activities they would be willing to give of their time and their talents for the church. It may include such diverse things as hosting people for a night, telling children's stories, or serving on various boards and committees of the church.

What is good about such a survey is that it allows members to identify areas in which they have a particular interest and to which they would be willing to give themselves with some degree of enthusiasm. Too often people are asked to do things for which they feel no talent or interest but respond out of duty or guilt. What would you really like to do for the church?

There is also the hope that such a survey will uncover some hidden talents. I have found that many members do unique and interesting things, but because they are quiet and unassuming they never receive any recognition or affirmation. How can these people be discovered and their talents made available to the congregation?

Sometimes the time and talent survey is designed to help deal with a particular problem, namely, certain members of the church seem to assume that they have a corner of control in particular areas. We have all known of congregations where one person was in the office as congregational chair for too many years. Maybe new talent can be uncovered through such a survey.

The time and talent survey offers the promise of new life,

new commitments, new involvement, new energy for a congregation. It is a way to make clear that Christian commitment within the community of faith involves more than money in the annual pledge and Sunday offering. People can give of themselves!

There are some dangers, however, in time and talent surveys, so let's look at that side to balance the picture. Compiling a time and talent survey involves considerable time and energy in itself, which is all right if it is used. But how many times have such surveys been done only to lie dormant and unused?

Often the final step in compiling the survey form is omitted, and that is to print multiple copies of the results so that they are available to the groups and people in the congregation who might use them. Lists on index cards or today on a computer in the office are not adequate. Type up that master list and make copies, and then pass them around.

The second problem is confusing the time and talent survey with gift discernment in the congregation. Time and talent surveys are what we say about ourselves. Gift discernment is what the congregation collectively says about us. And they are not necessarily the same.

That brings me to the third problem, and it is probably the most critical. A covenant is implied in the time and talent survey, and the covenant is this: If I volunteer my time or my talent, someone will ask me to do something in line with what I have volunteered to do.

But what if that doesn't happen? What if no one asks? What happens to an already fragile self-esteem? And how does the unasked volunteer now feel about his or her congregation?

Anyone who has dealt with a time and talent survey knows that some people see themselves capable of doing things of which others rightly or wrongly believe them to be incapable. So they go on being ignored.

On the whole, time and talent surveys can still be useful. But I would not do it every year in a congregation for fear that the dangers might overtake the positive potential.

January 5, 1989

10. Multiple Staff Churches Face Hurdles

During the course of the evening one denominational group reported having done a survey of multiple staff congregations. They discovered that 80 percent of these were having serious staff conflicts!

In my early years of ministry I yearned for the opportunity to be part of a ministry team, where I wouldn't have to be responsible for everything or be expected to preach every Sunday. After all, if there were at least two of us, we ought to not only double the pleasure but also double the work output. Neither is true.

When I came into my present job I found in the office a book titled *Let's Talk About Church Staff Relationships,* by Ronald W. Wiebe and Bruce A. Rowlison. The cover of the book has a picture of six happy male clergy (obviously a very large congregation by most standards). With Bible prominently in hand, winsome smiles suggesting love and cooperation, and hands folded in a gesture of piety, the picture suggests the ideal model of a church staff as they pose on the steps in front of their church door.

The back cover of the book pictures the same group of clergy standing in the same pose, but the camera now is inside the church and we see the six happy male clergy from the backside. This picture tells a different story. In place of the Bible, an issue of *Playboy is* stuck in the hip pocket of one clergyman. Another holds a knife and is stabbing a colleague in the back. Still another is picking the pocket of a trusting colleague, and another is paying off a colleague who holds the offering plate behind his back. Does the front or the back contain the true picture?

For some time I have felt that we have been rushing headlong into multiple staff ministries with inadequate preparation and even less understanding of the complexity of the issues we will encounter. It's not a happy scene when you know the picture from the inside.

I was in a meeting recently involving a diverse group of denominations. During the course of the evening one denominational group reported having done a survey of multiple staff congregations. They discovered that 80 percent of these were having serious staff conflicts!

Before unduly frightening pastors and congregations moving toward multiple staff, let me tell you the other side of the story. My second congregation was a multiple staff experience, and by and large it was a positive experience, though with several significant footnotes to the contrary.

I must pay credit to my first colleague, Esko Loewen, with whom I served in a co-pastor role for six years. He helped me to survive in a situation for which I was not prepared. He was a good mentor and colleague who always treated me with equality, though 20 years my senior.

There were still times of conflict and in retrospect I know now that I did not always act appropriately in this relationship. But it was good, and I believe that we both survived because we were together in a situation where neither of us would have made it alone.

Other colleagues came and went in the years that followed. There were many good times for us and for the church. Best were those with whom one felt a mutual respect and pride in the work of each other.

In retrospect, I came into a multiple staff situation with much idealism, but totally unprepared educationally or emotionally for the complexity which I was to encounter. What I know now I had to learn on the job. I'm glad that we as a church are maturing to where we know we must do better to help pastors and congregations who are large enough to need multiple staff ministerial leadership.

February 2, 1989

25

11. Dispelling Myths of Multiple Staffs

I am convinced that in most healthy situations there will be a clear designation of authority coupled with a sincere commitment to the equality of relationships.

When most of us approach the idea of multiple staff in our congregations, we bring a great deal of hope and idealism with our expectations. It turns out that we often forget both the reality of human sin and what might be realistic expectations regarding people working together. Here are several myths I have learned.

Myth No. 1: If we had more willing volunteers in our large church, we would not need to hire additional staff. The reality is just the opposite. If you want more people to become involved in volunteering in your congregation, you will need more staff, not less, to coordinate that energy.

Myth No. 2: By hiring a second pastor to our church staff, we will double the output of work accomplished. It's never true, and for good reasons. When two people work together, there is some inevitable overlap. Some meetings, though hopefully not too many, will call for them both to be there. Then they will need to take significant time to be in communication with each other if they are not to end up pulling in two directions. At best, you can expect $1\frac{3}{4}$ the output with two people.

Myth No. 3: It is quite acceptable for both pastors to routinely visit members in the hospital on the same day. I am amazed how often I hear of this happening. Laity intuitively know that double visits suggest that their pastors are either not in good communication or inefficient or both. Pastors on a team must develop a clear plan of activity to make responsible use of time.

Myth No. 4: Since we are all equal in the sight of God, pastoral staff members should all be equals in their positions. This issue is probably the primary cause for staff dissension. I am convinced that in most healthy situations there will be a clear designation of authority coupled with a sincere commitment to the equality of relationships. What we often get today turns this on its head so that we end up with equalitarian structures and authoritarian relationships. That is a formula for disaster.

Myth No. 5: Titles are unimportant. The truth is that titles communicate identity. They help in defining boundary clarity for both the pastoral staff and for the congregation. Titles are also a problem, especially for those in assistant positions.

I am convinced that we will go through cycles of titles which are descriptive of the task (i.e., youth pastor) and those which are descriptive of position (i.e., associate pastor). When one set is no longer acceptable we shift to the other, and so the cycle continues. Let me also voice my dismay at what I consider title inflation with the use of lead pastor or senior pastor. I much prefer just the title pastor and the more traditional associate/assistant pastor.

Myth No. 6: We have a large church and have never needed more than one pastor for 500 members. How does a congregation determine the size of its pastoral staff today? What I have learned about this issue comes from Lyle Schaller. First of all, he says, one should figure not on the basis of membership but by the average worship attendance, which is a much more realistic figure regarding the size of a congregation.

The second issue one must ask is whether you want to have adequate pastoral staff to maintain the status quo or if you want to plan for growth. The basic formula is one pastor for the first 200 in average Sunday worship, and an additional pastor for each additional 100 in attendance to maintain the present program of the congregation. To plan for growth there should be an additional pastoral staff position added.

Thus a congregation with an average of 400 in worship attendance should have three pastors for maintenance, and four for growth, plus the needed secretarial and custodial support staff.

These are only a few of the issues that the larger congregations must consider when they move toward becoming a multiple staff congregation. It is a highly complex issue, and often our assumptions turn out to be wrong.

February 16, 1989

12. Who Selects Hymns for Worship?

If you never sing songs of the heart, you also are missing something important and valuable to faith.

"Who chooses the hymns we sing in worship each Sunday?" As a pastor I was always surprised when somebody asked that question. Wasn't it obvious that the pastor does that?

That was never a question for me, although it maybe should have been. From childhood I knew how choosing hymns was done. On Saturday night my father would call the song leader to inform him of the hymns my father had chosen.

That was a simpler time. There was no bulletin nor did there seem to be any need for the organist to know. But at least the song leader was told the night before.

Well, things changed in my ministry. We now have bulletins, and so hymns need to be selected in time for the printing. And now the organist wants to know not the night before or even several days before. She wants to know weeks in advance so other music may be chosen accordingly.

I had to learn and adjust, and it was good discipline for me. But the "tape" from my childhood was not completely changed. It was the pastor who chose the hymns.

I still defend that practice. Most pastors I know select the hymns carefully and with a great deal of thought. They look for hymns that will fit into the overall theme of the worship or the sermon. Most pastors keep careful record in a master hymnal of when each hymn has been sung, thus avoiding undue repetition and encouraging diversity of selection.

Hymns are integral to the worship not only in the theme and content but also to the flow and development of the service. In the opening hymn I looked for strong hymns of faith in God, hymns by which we could begin worship with the affirmation of the one who reigns and rules in this oftentimes unruly universe. These were hymns of the community of faith with emphasis on the "we" of the community.

In the middle of worship I looked for hymns that were more reflective or meditative, reflecting life in the Spirit. They were more personal. I have never agreed with those who claimed that hymns which focused on the individual or the "I" were inappropriate in worship. To me the issue was one of balance between the individual and the community.

The hymns at the close of the worship should be hymns of dedication and commitment, often in response to the theme of the sermon. Again they should be strong statements of discipleship to the Christ who calls us to follow him.

Here are some additional things I learned and am still learning: I now know that I tended to be too narrow in believing that the best text to fit my theme was the most important factor in the selection of hymns. I now know that familiarity with the hymn is more important to most members of the congregation. We enjoy singing the familiar. People are willing to learn new hymns, especially if we help them to do so, but not every Sunday and certainly not with every hymn. I wish I had understood that earlier in my ministry.

Pastors also want to choose hymns that they believe are theologically correct. Members of the congregation are less concerned with that. I have learned that I, too, can sing things which I could not recite as creedal statements.

That is not to say that we should be unconcerned about the theology of hymns. Hymns are, after all, powerful shapers of our theology and therefore deserve careful selection. But I can now sing with at least occasional enthusiasm some of the so-called gospel songs.

If gospel songs are all you sing, you are missing a great deal. But if you never sing songs of the heart you also are missing something important and valuable to faith.

I also learned that even though I assumed responsibility for the selection of the hymns as pastor, I could also benefit by involving some others in the selection process occasionally. Choir directors, organists, and others are often anxious to make suggestions. Ask them.

March 2, 1989

13. Worship Has Lost Its Sense of Awe

Worship contains both our humanity and that persistent sense of awe in a universe so vast and wondrous.

I confess that I cannot define what worship is. I do not know how to create a worship experience for anyone else. Furthermore, I acknowledge that what is meaningful worship to me may not be to you. You could say the same in return.

I do not want to pretend that there is only one right way to worship, except that which our Lord said would be "in spirit and in truth."

Nevertheless, it seems to me that in much of our public worship today we have lost the sense of awe. We speak about the presence of God, but I find it often difficult to believe the truth of our words. So often God seems neither transcendent as the Almighty who reigns over the universe nor imminent as the loving and compassionate God who is near in our need.

We have domesticated God, tamed what the poet Francis Thompson called "the Hound of heaven." Whatever god is present is one whom we have well under control, a god on our leash. Whatever god is present is one designed to make us feel good about ourselves and comfortable about our world.

Don't get me wrong. I believe in the necessity of self-esteem. I believe that God does love this wild and wicked world. And I believe that the Spirit does draw near to us with God's compassionate presence.

But I seldom sense any intensity of desire in public worship to be drawn toward a God of mystery, majesty, and grace. The sense of wonder seems gone. In its place we have substituted an easy certainty that God is on our side.

Perhaps the pendulum has swung too far in much of our contemporary church worship. The dominant change in worship in the last decades has been that we have sought to reestablish a sense of community in our worship experience. Some of that has been necessary and good. We do know God in the midst of our brothers and sisters in Christ as we share our common life.

But somehow with all our announcements for the coming week, with all our introductions, sometimes contrived to convince ourselves that we are a friendly church, and with all our extended informal sharing times, I go away feeling as though our so-called worship has been an exercise in human relationships.

Important though that may seem, I leave wondering where we are in relation to the divine presence among us. Is there anyone else who feels at times that we have created a worship structured only on the horizontal and lost any concern about that worship which seeks to reach out and to be found within the vertical?

Christianity has always best understood itself as a profound exercise in faith. To exercise that faith in a perplexing and sometimes crazy world demands that we reach up toward the Almighty God whose presence among us always remains a mystery.

Worship contains our certainties and our doubts. Worship contains our affirmations and our questions. Worship contains our experiences of abandonment and our experiences of God's presence. Worship contains our understanding and that which remains unclear. Worship contains both our humanity and that persistent sense of awe in a universe so vast and wondrous.

I began by saying that I do not know how to create such an experience of worship. I do know that my own preparation has something to do with whether I am ready for worship. I do know that those who lead us in our worship make a difference. We feel the spiritual mystery at the core of their lives.

I also know that beauty and truth come close to each other. I know we cannot create God's presence with all our fine planning for worship. But I also know we can prevent any possibility for it by our failure to take seriously our need for wonder.

April 6, 1989

14. How Long Should a Pastor Stay?

In the early years the burden is to justify leaving. As the years move on, the burden shifts to justify staying.

How long should a pastor stay in a congregation? Most of the time we avoid even asking that question for fear that we might be suggesting to our pastor that it's time to leave. There is no single right answer. Indeed there are many answers to fit many situations. Here are some of my thoughts and observations.

We ought to begin with setting our goal toward longer pastorates, in the range of eight to 12 years. There is an emerging consensus that the most significant years of ministry for a pastor begin after the fourth to sixth year. Does it really take that long to earn the necessary trust? Apparently so!

Some of our most competent pastors have decided to serve in 10-year cycles, giving them three to four different ministry experiences in a lifetime. Such pastors will make a transition about every 10 years, knowing it is far better to move when all is positive and going well.

Pastors need to consider many factors today. Children, of course, must be taken into consideration. I fondly remember my father turning down a significant opportunity so I could complete my high school.

Even more complex today is the part a spouse plays in this decision. Pastors' spouses are often professionals in their own right and don't always easily or willingly move.

Also to be considered is the congregation's place in its development. Given our modern mobility (the average person moves every four years), some congregational members move so often that the long-term pastor may be the only stable factor.

One pastor shared with me his struggle with this decision several years ago. He had led that congregation into a new era of change and growth. His ministry was at its peak and overwhelmingly positive. Despite this, he chose to leave knowing how essential and yet how difficult it would be for him to lead that same congregation into the next phase of growth. Recent contact with that congregation tells me that the new pastor is doing exactly what the previous pastor knew was needed but would have been nearly impossible for him.

Over the life cycle of a pastorate, the question pastors should ask themselves gradually shifts from "Why would I leave? " to "Why should I stay?" In other words, in the early years the burden is to justify leaving. As the years move on, the burden shifts to justify staying.

This is particularly true when one moves beyond the 12th year in a pastorate. One's ministry may remain positive, but what happens to the congregation when change finally comes? And what might that congregation experience with new leadership, recognizing the limitations all of us have?

Then there is the issue of the pastor's own growth and development. Many who have made transitions when that decision was difficult bear witness to the revitalization that new places and new challenges in ministry bring.

I am grateful to be in a vocation in which occasional transition is expected. I have been greatly enriched by the experiences, relationships, and personal growth which have come to me because of these transitions in ministry.

April 20, 1989

15. Say It Again So They Don't Forget

In my more naive years, I assumed that if something was announced once in any form, that ought to be sufficient.

"Well, what shall we do this evening?" asked father, who had just come home from a hard day at the office. "It's just turned to daylight savings time and I could mow the yard. And the national finals of the basketball tournament are on TV; I don't want to miss that."

"But Tom, don't you remember that there is a meeting at church tonight for all the parents of teenagers? We can't miss that. Susan is more important to us than some ball game!" mother said with emotion in her voice.

"I didn't know that was planned for tonight."

"Well, don't you read the bulletin? And we received a special letter a week ago from the church to remind us how important it is for us to be there."

"I read through the whole bulletin—all eight pages of it—during the prelude yesterday, and I don't remember seeing anything about that," replied father.

If something like the above brief dialogue has ever happened in your home, you are not alone. Communication is a persistent problem for most of us. How can the church work effectively at communication in an age of information overload?

In my more naive years, I assumed that if something was announced once in any form, that ought to be sufficient. After all, intelligent people should listen the first time. Since then my own life has grown more complex. In fact, just this morning I missed an office birthday party at coffee because the one time I was told about it was not sufficient to get it on my calendar or into my consciousness.

Redundant communication is the new term to say that we

must work at repeating several times and in several different forms the information we want to get through to people. One time is seldom enough.

Communication is the oil of good relationships. If we want people to feel a part of the church we need to share with them as much information as possible. With good communication, trust is built. With good communication, congregational members feel that they belong and are a part of the action.

That's why churches need bulletins and sometimes newsletters. That's why special things call for special attention on Sunday mornings. In our church we have an occasional "Kingdom Report," which may highlight a service project, or someone might share a significant event in the community. When the stewardship campaign is about to begin, a group will prepare a humorous skit so that everyone there will know what to expect.

I know that information must be repeated if we are concerned about communicating with the whole congregation effectively. However, I do have two pet peeves.

I remember attending a service in one congregation where the printed bulletin announcements were literally read back to the congregation. It may have been redundant communication, but it was also an insult to the intelligence of the members. More creativity than that is called for.

My second pet peeve has to do with the length of the bulletin. There is not a clear correlation between the amount of information in the bulletin and the amount of communication that occurs. Sometimes the more that is printed the less one can expect to be read and absorbed. Good editorial discipline in being clear and concise is a gift to be valued, especially in church bulletins.

May 4, 1989

16. Use Three Years for Better Efficiency

What are the cycles by which you order your life and activities as a church?

A year is a year is a year; is it not so? It begins January 1 and ends December 31. That is indeed a year, according to our Western Gregorian calendar as reformed by Pope Gregory XIII in 1582.

There are, of course, many other calendars by which other cultures and peoples live. According to the Jewish calendar this is not 1989 but 5750; the Islamic calendar says we are in the year 1410.

But what is the calendar by which your congregation lives? Of course, you use the Gregorian calendar to date the events of the church. However, the question I am after is: What are the cycles by which you order your life and activities as a church?

The answer is still not easy. Although some churches don't pay much attention (perhaps we should do more) to the church liturgical year, we ought to at least be aware that the Christian calendar begins a new year every Advent season as we prepare to celebrate the birth of the Messiah, and it ends with the season of Trinity in November.

But what is the effective year by which we order our lives and by which we order the program of the church? May I suggest still another answer?

Most of us personally and most institutions of our society order themselves more by the school year than by the calendar year. The practical beginning of the year is in September with a significant closure at the end of May. The cycle rounds out with a distinctly different interim time called summer, and our year ends in August.

What are the implications of this for how you function as a congregation? Typically congregations hold their annual meetings to conduct the business of the church sometime in January. Reports are given and elections are held. And the cycle begins again.

But have you ever thought about what that means in terms of the church's program and how people give leadership to it? In December we're too busy with Christmas and the year is almost ended; new people will be elected soon. In January the elections take place, so now we must appoint new committees to get started. In February we try to orient new people to their responsibilities so they can function effectively.

What has just happened? In the middle of our effective year of activity running from September through August, we have just consumed three months to effect the transition of leadership. It's a wonder as much is accomplished as happens.

So what are alternatives? How about having the church function on three different years all at once? Would that be too confusing? I know it has worked.

1. Leave the fiscal year to follow the calendar year, and still hold a congregation meeting in January to deal primarily with financial issues. Hear financial reports and approve a new budget.

2. Allow the church education year for Sunday school to follow the school year; life transitions can still be in sync.

3. Make the church year for those who are chosen for certain positions to run from June through May. Annual reports and elections can be held in late April or early May as things naturally wind down. New committees and boards can organize and plan for the coming year during the summer. The transition time is then linked to the time of somewhat reduced or altered church routines rather than in the midst of what is the middle of our effective year of scheduled activities.

This works effectively and is not nearly as confusing as it may sound. It also pushes the congregation to meet and talk about the work of the church more than just once a year. How about planning for a spring, a fall, and a winter meeting of the congregation?

May 18, 1989

17. You Can Cancel the Summer Slump

We don't take a vacation from God or from the church, but we do need to vary our pace and our style through the cycle of the year.

When I was a pastor, I found the summer to be one of the happiest times of the church year. We planned for a distinct change of pace and style. Summer called for some new and different ways to plan our worship and our life as a congregation.

Then several years ago my wife and I attended a workshop in a United Methodist Church in Los Altos, California. We were there in midsummer and discovered that the congregation had as one of its themes "Cancel the Summer Slump." I like that.

Several myths are perpetuated about congregations regarding the summer season. One notion is that people not only take family vacations in summer, they also take vacations from church and presumably from God.

Another myth is that financial support of the congregation declines dramatically in summer. To both notions, I say: Cancel the summer slump.

For years the notion prevailed that our financial giving declined dramatically during the summer. After all, by the end of the summer we were consistently at the bottom of our financial resources to pay the routine bills of the church. It turns out that a more accurate analysis of the facts did not substantiate this myth.

When we studied our giving over several years, we learned that our average per month giving was nearly equal from February through September. The low level of resources by the end of the summer was really a cash-flow problem, reflecting the larger giving cycle of the entire year.

Giving is low in January, levels off from February through September and increases from October through December. The natural low in the cash flow happens to coincide with the end of summer and should not cause panic.

But what about the gathered life and worship of the congregation during the summer? How can one cancel the summer slump feeling there?

Acknowledge that summer is different and should be planned accordingly. We don't take a vacation from God or from the church, but we do need to vary our pace and our style through the cycle of the year. Over the years, several things can be done to accomplish that change.

In our congregations, the choirs do take a summer vacation, but that gives a wonderful opportunity to do some other things. Various Sunday school classes might be made responsible for the anthem, giving opportunity for members of these classes to meet for a potluck supper before rehearsing for the following Sunday!

We also tried to involve the children and youth of the congregation during the summer. Use the musical talents they are developing for solos or in groups. Sometimes they might play for the offertory in addition to the anthem.

As a pastor I also used the summer to plan a more unusual series of sermons. Several ideas I used were the shorter and lesser-known books of the Bible, sermons based on the texts of hymns, and a series about the historic heresies of Christianity and how we can discern truth from error.

One year I did a sermon series on the Apocrypha, those valued and instructive books that have been preserved but not included in most Protestant Bibles. I'm sure there are many other creative ways to plan for preaching that will help cancel the summer slump.

Shorten the bulletin. Involve more people in leadership. Sing hymns you might tend to avoid but which are old-time favorites of members in the congregation. Cancel the summer slump.

June 1, 1989

18. Professionalism Can Be a Good Thing

When I think of being professional, what comes to mind first is a high commitment to excellence and competence.

"Professional" has become a bad word in many circles, especially when it is applied to the pastor. I disagree with that assessment. I believe most pastors would benefit from an increased sense of being professionals in who they are and what they do.

Before I explain, we must try to understand why some think that being a professional pastor is a problem. The negative expression of being professional comes when persons become obsessed with the importance of their positions and their titles, and seek recognition of their importance.

Another aspect of being professional which is perceived negatively has to do with self-seeking financial gain—professionals supposedly are money-grabbing persons who will take all they can get from the rest of us. Finally, professionals are perceived as those who set themselves above and over others, and who are accountable to no one but themselves.

Whenever pastors engage in any of the above and do so in the name of being professional, I, too, would join in the rejection of professionalism. In fact, such attitudes and actions are quite unprofessional, and represent distortions of the kind of leadership which we seek in the church or anywhere in society.

So what does it mean to be a professional? A professional pastor? When I think of being professional, what comes to mind first is a high commitment to excellence and competence. This means pursuing both the best initial training available as well as a high commitment to continuing education.

Professionals do not just seek to get by with whatever they can; rather they seek to develop the God-given gifts for ministry to the highest level of skill of which they are capable. There was a song popular in church circles in my youth, "Give of Your Best to the Master." That's the spirit and attitude of competent pastors which the church is calling for in our day.

Second, the true professional understands and embodies the idea that being in leadership always means that one is the servant of others, and the servant of the institution or church to which you have been called.

Being called into ministry is a rare and holy privilege which is not to be grasped after but is to be accepted with humility and gratitude. Pastors who would be leaders must begin as the disciples of Jesus from whom they have learned what servanthood is all about.

Third, being a professional means having a clear identity about one's role within the community we call the church. It is to acknowledge and accept that, as a leader, one has a unique representational role. One is not just a member like everyone else.

Part of that representational role is claiming the mystery of authority without becoming authoritarian. Part of that role is accepting a priestly identity through which the grace of God may be shared.

The best definition of being a true professional is one I learned from my former colleague, Harold Bauman, who in turn credited the following to Wayne Oates: "The person is trained to do the work; the person is paid so they have time to do the work; the person is accountable to a group for the quality of work they do." I like that, particularly the last point on accountability.

Professionals are not lone rangers, operating in isolation and independence. All persons worthy of being termed professionals accept that they are held accountable by both their ministry peers and the entire community they serve for their ethical standards and overall competence.

September 17, 1989

19. Inclusive Words Heighten Worship

I knew that I had been in the presence of a living God who is still at work within our world and within the church.

"Men of God, arise and sing." With those words our associate pastor, who is a woman, sat down. It was a dramatic moment as the men of the congregation stood and sang:
"Rise up, O men of God!
Have done with lesser things;
Give heart and soul and mind and strength
To serve the King of kings."
"Lift high the cross of Christ!
Tread where His feet have trod
As brothers of the Son of man
Rise up, O men of God!"

With other men spread around our church sanctuary, my heart thrilled to sing this stirring hymn. What an inspired idea by which to use a hymn loaded with male imagery; let the men sing it!

I am committed to the increasing use of inclusive language in all our conversation and especially in our worship. I have been working to change old patterns of male exclusiveness in my own speaking, using terms that reflect our need and desire to include all persons, men and women, young and old, within the family of God. Change is not easy, and sometimes I fall back into old patterns.

Change is especially hard in our beloved rituals of the church, such as in our hymns. But by now I have learned that many of our hymns have actually been improved by the use of more inclusive texts.

This change will come slowly. I still resent the regular suggestion that we should change this word and that word before the singing of each hymn. I can never remember or anticipate where that change is to occur without losing the larger meaning of the hymn. But where the printed text can be appropriately altered to a more inclusive vision of Christ's church, let it happen.

Change is also coming to the text of Scripture which will reflect our more inclusive ways of speaking. Within the next year the New Revised Standard Version will be available to the public. The changes being made are conservative, well within the appropriate guidelines of careful and honest translation.

God will not be changed by human translation of Scripture, but we have changed in response to the inclusive visions of Ephesians 3:5-6: "In former generations this mystery was not made known to humankind, as it has now been revealed to his holy apostles and prophets by the Spirit: that is, the Gentiles have become fellow heirs, members of the same body, and sharers in the promise in Christ Jesus through the gospel" (NRSV).

We had a second surprise in our worship that Sunday. The men had sung the old hymn: "Rise Up, O Men of God." This was followed by the story for children. Then our bulletin called for another hymn—new words with a familiar tune: "Rise Up, O Saints of God. " Together as one congregation we stood with our pastors, both male and female, to sing:

"Rise up, O saints of God!
From vain ambitions turn
Christ rose triumphant that your hearts
With nobler zeal might burn."
"Commit your hearts to seek
The paths which Christ has trod
And quickened by the Spirit's power,
Rise up, O saints of God."

The double surprise of these two hymns, both appropriately sung by those represented in their texts, was about all the worship I could tolerate in my limited spirit. I knew that I had been in the presence of a living God who is still at work within our world and within the church. It was indeed a holy moment.

September 7, 1989

20. Wise Use of Time Vital for Pastors

It is my strong belief that the typical pastor's week should be in the range of 50 hours on the job.

Pastors live with a paradox in relation to time. Almost no other vocation gives to an employee as much freedom and discretionary time as is given to pastors. But also, almost no other vocation is as demanding in expectations of time and availability as is a pastor.

My wife, a nurse, is expected to work every other weekend; as a pastor I was on duty every Sunday. There are others who work evenings, but pastors are expected to be in the office also in the morning and on visitation often in the afternoons. Many couples reserve Friday or Saturday night for personal activities; during certain times of the year those evenings were taken with wedding rehearsals and ceremonies.

Many pastors have been on vacation, only to experience an urgent call to return home for a funeral. Then there is the call in the middle of the night to come quickly to the hospital.

I don't want pastors playing martyr on the issue of the demands on their time, but it is easy to understand why some do. As I observe not only pastors but other professionals as well, I see that they all demand more than the 40-hour week.

How then can pastors be fair to themselves and their families, and still be responsible in the use of their time? Let me share several things I learned.

Plan and work ahead! In my first years of ministry I found Saturday to loom as an enormous burden. I cleaned the church for that little extra income. I had to do the bulletin. And finally there was the sermon to finish.

It didn't take too many Saturdays like that for me to figure out that things would have to change. The most significant change was to make it my goal to complete the sermon on Thursday, which always provided for backup time if necessary.

Don't act busy or rushed, even if you are. I wanted to communicate to people that they were not imposing on my other important agenda; *they* were what was important to me.

It is easy for pastors to suggest in not-so-subtle ways that people are an intrusion. When we do that we have lost what servanthood is all about. If other commitments have been made, suggest an alternative time and people will be most understanding.

Compensate when the demands of ministry take unusual time. When the evening meetings came too often, I was not at the office by 8 a.m. Pastors, for their own well-being, should have one and a half days off every week. For many that includes all day Monday. I found Saturday more satisfying; I have known others to take Thursday.

It is my strong belief that the typical pastor's week should be in the range of 50 hours on the job. Stories of pastors who work 60, 70, and even 80 hours a week suggest to me inefficiency, poor management, poor self-discipline, masochism, or the need to look important and indispensable!

Another useful method for judging the pastor's time involvement is to consider each morning, each afternoon, and each evening as a unit of time. In that case the typical full-time pastor should invest 12 to 14 units each week.

As for evenings, I learned that I could cope with three evenings a week invested in the church; when that moved to four, the emotional and physical toll was too much. Except for weddings and emergencies, Friday evenings were never scheduled with church groups.

Ultimately pastors must assume responsibility about how they develop their schedule and use of time; we can't expect others to do that for us. That means being available and responsive to situations of need. That also means learning when and how to set the limits, and occasionally to say "no."

September 21, 1989

46

21. Pursuing Excellence in Ministry

Pastors who strive toward excellence bring enthusiasm and energy to their work, with the result that they truly enjoy what they are doing.

It was Sunday evening at the end of another hot Kansas summer day. My wife Bernice, who is a nurse and thus must work every other weekend, had an exceptionally strenuous and long day at the hospital. It was clear that it would be a quiet evening at home.

But what should I do? I'm not much of a TV watcher and I was weary of reading the too-large Sunday newspaper. I picked up a new book anyhow, thinking I might read a few pages. Instead, I grew excited and animated, reading occasional lines and paragraphs out loud to Bernice. This was great stuff!

Pursuing Excellence in Ministry by Daniel V. Biles may not be the chosen reading for leisure on a hot summer Sunday by most pastors, but I hope that many of them will read it come Monday morning. After reading *In Search of Excellence* by Tom Peters (a study of outstanding management in the business world and also well worth reading; my son gave it to me for Christmas a couple of years ago), Daniel Biles asked himself what the church and pastors might learn from Peters about excellence in ministry.

He set out to do a study of Lutheran congregations and pastors who were excellent in ministry. What was it that enabled them to pursue excellence? The book is his report.

Though Biles is clear that both the pastor and the congregation must be committed to excellence, and both must be actively involved in ministry, he sees the pastor as the central person in defining the tone, the vision, the commitment to healthy and vibrant congregational life.

Pastors who strive toward excellence bring enthusiasm and energy to their work, with the result that they truly enjoy what they are doing.

"Vision was the word used with almost boring repetition by clergy and laity alike in describing the leadership role of the pastor. Demonstrate a commitment to excellence in preaching, worship, teaching, outreach, and pastoral care, and people will take notice."

But leadership is not just this public role in ministry; some of the hard work that makes for excellence consists of learning on the job the skills of administration. Through administration the pastor translates the vision expressed in preaching into action and thus enables the congregation to implement the vision.

What should be the focus of a ministry that pursues excellence? Biles answers that it is in returning to the basics of faith: worship, education (especially adult education—Jesus taught adults and played with children while we teach children and play with adults!), care, and outreach. The constant commitment to quality is a theme that runs through his research.

I have one argument to pick with Biles, and that is his attack on professionalism, which he defines as "an elitist spirit in the ordained ministry." He is right, having defined professionalism in that way; elitism is a real and genuine danger.

There is another understanding of professionalism, however, which is not negative and which we need. Indeed it has to do with this commitment to excellence and competence within the structures of accountability. It also has to do with a clarity of one's identity as a minister and an acceptance of that role.

Incidentally, I didn't finish the book that night, but I did get up at 5:30 in the morning to do so!

December 1, 1988

22. Pastor's Spouse: Not an Easy Role

My hope is that we, as a church and as congregations, will be able to affirm spouses who choose any of these options and the variations within them.

I remember Lyle Schaller once saying that two things are essential to a positive experience in ministry. I've forgotten his first point, but the second essential was a happy, positive spouse!

I don't think he meant that as a command that all pastors should be married to be successful. He meant that if a pastor is married, it is essential that the spouse feels positive about the relationship with the husband or wife and with the congregation.

I'm sure that many pastors would join me in bearing witness to the wonderful supporting relationship which an affirming spouse can bring to ministry. Receiving trust helps to confirm fidelity. Being the helpful listener who retains absolute confidentiality helps to build trust and enlarges what can be shared. Offering the gentle suggestions and the occasional challenge from alternative perspectives helps to enlarge the pastor's vision. The list goes on and on.

The role of the pastor's spouse is not an easy one, however. It has never been and it still is not. The last 30 years have seen a great deal of change for the pastor's spouse, but the changes have only increased the complexity of that role—not made it easier.

Today there are more options, both personally and vocationally, for the pastor's spouse. I have found it helpful to identify what these options are, and to consider how each of them can and should be viewed positively.

First there is the traditional pastor's wife. (Yes, I used "wife" intentionally here. I don't know of any pastor's husband, of which we have an increasing number, who would fill this role.) The pastor's wife fills a unique and special role alongside of her pastor husband, growing out of both her gifts and the fact that they are married to each other.

She may carry extra responsibilities in the church. Often she will accompany her husband on visitation. Though she receives no financial remuneration, she is perceived by all as a part of the pastoral team. She offers this service to Christ and the church because she chooses to do so and finds great fulfillment in it.

When this is done well and when the commitment to it is voluntary, it serves to the blessing of all, and churches love her and bless her for it. The danger is that they also come to expect it of all pastor's spouses.

Today I find that women who have and are serving their Lord and the church in this first option are almost apologetic and on the defensive; they feel that other pastor's spouses look down on them as old-fashioned. That is too bad. I for one want to be on record as affirming the pastor's wife who finds spiritual fulfillment in this unique and special role as a form of her ministry.

The second major option today is for the couple who is both trained and committed to serve together in pastoral ministry. Both wife and husband are seen as pastors; both receive financial support. This is another unique and special form which deserves our clear affirmation. It is a highly complex and very special form of the co-pastor model. For now let me be clear in support of this model for spouses in ministry together. It is neither superior nor inferior to the first option, but is another form chosen by some.

The third option, and probably the one most prevalent today, is the pastor's spouse who chooses the role of a lay person in the congregation. Whether male or female, they often have a profession of their own and thus are employed outside of the home. Clearly this puts limitations on church involvement, but it also gives them the freedom to choose how and when and where they will be involved in the church.

Debbie Fast did a survey of pastor's spouses for the *Mennonite Reporter*. She writes: "Most pastor's spouses see themselves in the same way as any other member of the congregation. They participate because of a commitment to the church, not because they are married to the pastor." Again, I give affirmation to this third model as well as to my own wife Bernice, who found her own place within it.

My hope is that we, as a church and as congregations, will be able to affirm spouses who choose any of these options and the variations within them. It is dangerous and unfair to put our expectations and perceptions on others whose vision for themselves and the church of Christ may be different from our own.

October 19, 1989

23. Help for Those with "Ears to Hear"

I have realized that to hear and understand what has been said is so valuable that the content of the message becomes almost secondary.

I received an interesting letter in the mail recently in response to this column. The writer shared an idea which I agree needs to be addressed. It has to do with hearing and understanding what is being said during worship.

There are, of course, two issues here. One has to do with spiritually hearing the word of the Lord and responding in faith to it. That is a problem for all of us, and it has something to do with that strange word of our Lord: "If you have ears to hear, then hear."

The other issue regarding hearing and understanding has to do with physically hearing and understanding what is being said. The writer of the above letter reported the following personal experience. He had been to six funerals recently, three of which he could understand very well what was being said. The other three were "not good at all," as he put it.

He went on to describe how so often the minister begins with a good volume, but as an important point is being made the voice grows more and more quiet (presumably for emotional effect!) so that those with hearing difficulty finally can't understand what has been said.

As a pastor I began to realize how important it is for persons to hear and understand, whether in worship or in a small group or over the buzz of many conversations during the fellowship time. Not to hear is to feel left out. To feel left out is to experience increasing frustration, alienation, isolation, and anger.

When I have imagined myself in the situation of those who have hearing difficulties, I have realized that to hear and understand what has been said is so valuable that the content of the message becomes almost secondary.

Ministers can do something about how they speak. We can learn to enunciate with clarity. Most of us could slow down so as not to run our words together, but you must also be careful not to lose others because of speaking too slowly. Find a good natural rhythm and speed. We can learn how to breathe properly so that our lungs can support our vocal cords without strain.

As a young pastor, I knew I needed to improve my diction and my speaking, generally. One year I went to the two-week summer pastor's conference at Princeton Seminary. Along with the theological and biblical lectures, they offered a speech workshop. With more than a little fear and uncertainty, I chose that option. For what I learned, I have been very grateful.

From the responses I have received over the years, I know that how one speaks in public settings makes a difference, especially to those whose hearing has begun to be a problem. Pastors who believe that they bear an important message for God must put energy into their voice equal to the exhortation of their thoughts and words.

This does not mean shouting. At least I tune out and turn off shouting in the church. Harold Moyer told me the story about a note scribbled in the margins of a certain preacher's sermon: "Weak point, shout louder."

What about the public address system? And what special aids are available today for the hearing impaired? Most of us remember the old hearing aids located in a few rows somewhere near the front of the church. Their cords were almost always tattered, as I remember, and they were probably more fun for children to play with than they were of genuine help to those with hearing loss. Certainly one was conspicuous when one used them.

Today, with all the modern technology, there are several new systems which allow persons who are hearing impaired to sit wherever they choose. From what I have been told, they really are much more effective and would be well worth some churches making the investment in a new system.

Finally, let me share an idea having to do with sight. From a congregation in Bluffton, Ohio, I learned about the option of using the modern office copier that enlarges to make several large-print copies of the church bulletin. As they put it: "We want those who have eyes to see."

November 2, 1989

24. A Church Is Not a Museum

The church building is for people, and organs are meant to be played.

Several months ago a friend stopped by my office. It was apparent that he was in considerable distress. Quickly his story came out.

Joe (not his real name) had recently retired. In his retirement Joe had decided to pursue what had been a longstanding avocation: he began taking private pipe organ lessons.

Years before, Joe had made an agreement with a local church-related institution to use their pipe organ for practice. In exchange he would keep an eye out for any repairs needed by the instrument, since there was no one else who used it consistently.

As things are wont to do, administrations changed. New people were in charge who knew neither Joe nor the longstanding agreement he had for the use of the organ. In fact they only learned about Joe's access to the organ when he reported the potential damage of a roof leak above the organ.

Without any personal contact, Joe soon received a letter informing him that he was no longer to have access to the organ at any time and that he was to cease using it immediately. He was crushed.

I helped Joe approach the administration personally (as they should have done with him). He told his story and, realizing the error of their judgment, the situation was resolved amicably. Joe is back at the organ.

This true story is an example of the mentality which churches and church institutions too often take toward their property. They view it as a museum to be maintained in perfect condition, so the people who contributed to it can see how nicely it is maintained and how no harm has come to it. Never mind if the building or the organ stands inaccessible to the needs of people and the community.

Now anyone who knows me well knows that I border on an obsession of keeping things attractive and in good condition. I believe it is appropriate and right to take pride in even material possessions. Churches and organs need to be well maintained, but they are not there as museums to be admired. *The church building is for people, and organs are meant to be played.*

Early in my ministry it occurred to me that church buildings and football stadiums are probably the most expensive structures in our society when one judges that by the hours they are in use each week or each year. I determined that, as far as I could influence things, the church building was to be used more than it was to be admired.

If something was broken and needed to be repaired or replaced, so be it. *The church building is for people, and organs are meant to be played.*

One of the needs we discovered in our Minneapolis, Minn., community was the need for a meeting place. The church building itself became part of our witness and mission, expressing our openness and desire to serve. In a setting where locked church doors are the norm, many found our doors open and the welcome mat out. *The church building is for people, and organs are meant to be played.*

In another congregation I was appalled to find a policy forbidding family reunions in the church facilities, even to members of that congregation. We reversed that policy to encourage its use for such purposes. Many of our churches have opened their doors during the week to provide a place for preschool services to children and families. We have learned that church facilities can be made to serve multiple purposes during the week and on Sunday. *The church building is for people, and organs are meant to be played.*

December 7, 1989

25. What Is Your Church's Identity?

What is the theology which gives strength to the faith of your members?

How do you respond to a member of your congregation who says the church is not meeting his or her spiritual needs?

It is impossible for every congregation to meet everyone's needs and expectations. Even in matters of faith we have become part of our consumer society, looking for the most satisfying personal experience.

It is important and positive that congregations reflect something of our natural and inevitable human diversity. In the friendly but competitive world, a congregation must clarify its identity and unique mission. What elements make up such an identity?

1. Worship style. This is probably the single most significant factor by which we respond to particular congregations. Some churches have free, spontaneous worship sharing among participants. Others worship in ways similar to the so-called high churches, with formal and structured liturgy. What worship style does your congregation use?

2. Music. Most of us would agree that music probably affects our sense of the spiritual more profoundly than anything else. What we would not agree on is the type of music that truly nourishes our spirits. For some it is the gospel songs; others find it in the scripture songs of recent vintage shown on a screen by an overhead projector; others find meaning in the contemporary, sensuous music of popular evangelicalism; still others find their spiritual nurture in the classical traditions of Bach, Mozart, and Beethoven.

When our high school girls sang an anthem of Schubert recently, I was in ecstasy. Not everyone would have agreed. What music defines your congregation?

3. Theology. We have been taught to believe that when we think about theology we must think in categories of right and wrong, orthodoxy or heresy. In fact, most of us practice our theology more in terms of meaningful and meaningless. What undergirds one person's faith appears to undermine others.

Most congregations reflect some overall consensus on the theology which supports and strengthens the faith of most members. But that consensus varies, even within denominations. What is the theology which gives strength to the faith of your members?

4. Social and ethical issues. All churches in North America address issues related to our society and our understanding of Christian ethics. But we do not speak to the same set of issues, nor do we speak to them in the same way. What social and ethical issues are spoken to in your congregation? Is it possible to benefit occasionally from alternative points of view? Would that be accepted in your congregation?

5. Special needs. Congregations are discovering they can specialize in responding to people's particular needs. Some work at family life ministries, others concentrate on singles. Still other congregations make a special point of ministering to the developmentally disabled, while others address the needs of the elderly. What unique ministry lies at the doorstep of your congregation?

6. Denominational loyalty. Working for a denominational office as I do, we wish every congregation would have 100 percent loyalty to who we are and what we represent. In fact, that is not the case. Some seem to have 30 percent loyalty and others 60 percent loyalty to their denominational identity. How much denominational loyalty does your congregation have?

These are some issues all congregations need to address in clarifying their identity and mission. There are other issues, such as attitude toward education, or level of cultural and national affirmation or antagonism. What other issues are important in clarifying your congregation's identity?

Having clarified the overarching identity, we should remember that it is important and helpful occasionally to reach outside and beyond ourselves to experience alternatives which are meaningful to others.

February 1, 1990

26. My Father, the Blind Evangelist

Blindness would never keep Dad from participating in life and enjoying the world.

February 12 (President Lincoln's birthday) was also the anniversary of my father's birth. John J. Esau was born on a farm near Mountain Lake, Minn., in 1900, the ninth child of immigrant parents from Russia.

When he was 3 years old, a stick was thrown, presumably by one of his brothers, and it struck young John in the eye. He had the sight of the other eye until, at age 27, through some relationship of the optic nerve to the original accident, he became totally blind. It was in the first year of my parents' marriage and the first year of his public ministry that this final blindness occurred—a blindness with which he would live for the next 53 years.

Having attended Moody Bible Institute, it was Dad's desire to serve within the Mennonite Church. What he experienced, however, was an initial rejection—how could a blind man be a pastor?

Eventually he found three small Christian Union congregations near Lima, Ohio, willing to risk a blind minister. He served all three those first years. He never let me forget his salary was $35 a month, with which he paid the rent and bought a car.

But when it came time for ordination, he sought that among his own Mennonite people. He was first ordained as a minister and then as an elder in a double ordination, which was the custom in those days.

But then the doors of opportunity began to open within the General Conference Mennonite world. For the next 40 years Dad gave himself as a pastor, an occasional interim pastor, and most of all as the traveling "blind evangelist." His parish was North America.

As I travel some of those same circuits in my own ministry role, I continue to meet persons who are anxious to tell me stories of their experiences with Dad. I cherish those opportunities.

The story I hear most often is the account of how a blind man uses a hammer to drive in a nail. Dad would request one person to bring 2 x 4's, another to bring a hammer and nails. The following night he would demonstrate a blind man's skills and make some appropriate moral interpretation. I am proud to still use the Plumb hammer which he was given by one congregation.

Much of my life has been influenced by my father. I responded in a faith commitment upon Dad's preaching. Later he baptized me. Then he officiated at our wedding. And finally, he led in my service of ordination.

This past summer when I saw the baseball movie *Field of Dreams,* I was overcome with emotion remembering how a blind father played catch with his son. I identified my location by voice so Dad knew where to throw the ball; then I rolled it back on the ground so he could hear it coming.

Then I remembered the time he took me to my first major league game in Chicago. Why would a blind man pay to *not* see a baseball game? Well, for some reason, he always chose to go to things he couldn't see.

We went to see Niagara Falls. We went to the Black Hills to see Mt. Rushmore. We went to see the sights of early America in and around Philadelphia. We climbed Pike's Peak. Blindness would never keep Dad from participating in life and enjoying the world.

I have received so much from my father, in addition to a receding hairline and a tendency toward being overweight. When I find myself sometimes saying inappropriate things, I remember he sometimes did the same.

But on the positive side, I want to embrace the positive attitude he had toward God, toward people, toward the world—all in the face of the overwhelming reality of his blindness. I want to embrace Dad's strong commitment to Christ, his desire to serve the church, and his love for and commitment to his Mennonite heritage. I want to embrace his strong convictions, balanced by an incredible sense of tolerance and understanding of others. I want to embrace his compassion and his generosity.

At my parents' wedding, in knowledge of Dad's impending blindness, they drew a "Scripture promise" from a box. To their astonishment it turned out to be Isaiah 42:16: "I will bring the blind by a way that they knew not; I will lead them in paths that they have not known; I will make darkness light before them, and crooked things straight. These things will I do unto them, and not forsake them." How true! How true!

February 15, 1990

27. Are You Covered by the Umbrella?

How, then, can the pastor be the umbrella to unify, rather than become the cause of conflict and disunity?

An insurance company uses the metaphor of the umbrella to symbolize the coverage they provide. The image is that all of one's insurance needs can be covered by this singular company.

The umbrella also is a helpful image of the pastor who meets the congregation's diverse needs. An effective pastor will serve the needs and interests of the entire congregation in a way that no one will feel excluded or marginalized. The pastor is a kind of umbrella providing full-service coverage.

This ideal model may seem unrealistic to some, yet I am convinced it is possible and essential to provide effective ministry in the average congregation.

Let's face it. Almost every congregation, whether large or small, contains a fair degree of diversity. That diversity includes differing theological understandings as well as differing spiritual expectations. Almost every congregation has considerable variation in educational levels, ranging from those with less than a high school education to those who have completed professional graduate degrees.

The congregations I served would be perceived on one end of the theological and educational spectrum, yet within these congregations there were committed members across the whole educational and theological range. Most of the time, most of our members felt included under the umbrella.

In our zeal for truth, the image of the umbrella has the appearance of being uncertain and compromising. Other metaphors we have used in a negative manner have been the fence rider or the pastor who has a finger lifted in the air to test which way the winds of the congregation are blowing. Both methods only serve

61

to go along to get along. Is this what I am suggesting with the image of the umbrella? I don't believe so, and I hope not.

Pastors must be and usually are persons of strong convictions and strong commitments. They can and should exercise leadership. It is inevitable that those convictions and commitments will not be felt with the same intensity by everyone in the congregation. How, then, can the pastor be the umbrella to unify, rather than become the cause of conflict and disunity?

The answer begins within the depths of the being and character of the pastor. Somewhere inside of us there must be a sincere belief with the hymn writer that "there's a wideness in God's mercy like the wideness of the sea."

It is an acknowledgment with Paul that we "understand only in part." This manifests itself in a nonjudgmental spirit which remains open to learning and growing, even as one helps others to learn and grow.

When I consider how patient God has been with me, when I consider how long and arduous has been my own growth and understanding with my full life and vocation involved in the process, then I become more patient and tolerant of others who carry other commitments and concerns.

Pastors can also extend the range of the umbrella by giving permission for differences. They can sometimes choose hymns not to their own liking, knowing that such hymns will meet the congregation's diverse spiritual needs.

Pastors can give positive affirmation to the reality of differing perceptions and conflicting understandings. And ultimately the pastor, whose own life is enlarged by entering deeply into the lives and experiences of others through spiritual ministry, will enlarge the umbrella's coverage over the congregation.

March 1, 1990

28. Inner Character Vital to Ministry

It is my own observation that pastors with perception problems often evidence strong left-brain function; they are highly rational and logical and wrong!

The primary issue in pastoral ministry today is not quantity but quality. While we are still concerned with finding an adequate number of pastoral leaders for our congregations, the far more critical question has to do with finding the truly creative and competent persons our congregations expect.

The issue is more complex than it seems. We know we can send students through schools to receive a theological education and work at skills development, but that is not enough. We can affirm persons for their gifts for ministry, but that is not enough. Information, knowledge, skills, and even gifts may fail the critical test of survival. What then do we seek?

The most significant writers on vocational competence and ministerial competence are pointing more in the direction of the being and character of the person rather than what they can do. Karen Lebacqz, in her excellent book *Professional Ethics,* writes: "It seems that character, not just function, is central to the professional role of clergy." She quotes Nolan Harman: "The Christian minister must be something before he can do anything . . . . His work depends on his personal character."

Likewise, Stephen Covey, in *The Seven Habits of Highly Effective People,* speaks about principle-centered leadership. He writes: "As a principle-centered person, you see things differently, and because you see things differently, you think differently, you act differently. Because you have a high degree of security, guidance, wisdom, and power that flows from a solid, unchanging core, you have the foundation of a highly pro-active and highly effective life."

Quoting Oliver Wendell Holmes: "What lies behind us and what lies before us are tiny matters compared to what lies within us." At its heart is it not a spiritual question—being in touch with oneself, with others, with the world, and with God?

Covey suggests that in order to clarify these central principles around which a pastor's life is given focus, it is helpful to begin with the end in mind. It is important for us to take the long-range view of the meaning and purpose of our lives so that we can live in the present effectively.

Who am I? What am I becoming by God's grace? Where am I going? And what are the qualities around the core of my being that will enable me to get there?

This sounds strangely similar to the Alcoholics Anonymous' principle of taking a vigorous inventory of one's own life. Perhaps they know something the rest of us need to learn.

Covey suggests that every person, and I would add every pastor, should write a personal mission statement. "Your mission statement becomes your constitution, the solid expression of your vision and your values. It becomes the criterion by which you measure everything else in your life."

This is not something done in an hour or two. It may take several months of processing and reflection, and it calls for ongoing review as life brings new understandings and insights.

I was particularly impressed with the way Covey discusses our ways of perceiving reality. He described how it is essential to use both sides of our brain. The left brain is more logical and verbal while the right side is more intuitive and creative. It is my own observation that pastors with perception problems often evidence strong left-brain function; they are highly rational and logical and wrong!

In contrast, Covey reports on the research of Charles Garfield, who became fascinated with peak performance. "One of the main things his research showed was that almost all of the world-class athletes and other peak performers are visualizers. They see it; they feel it; they experience it before they actually do it. They begin with the end in mind."

March 15, 1990

64

29. Change Habits, Beat Time Shortage

The real challenge is not to manage time but to manage ourselves.

My favorite cartoon series is called "Frank and Ernest" by Bob Thaves. It is the ongoing saga of two rather down-and-out, good-for-nothing men called Frank and Ernest. If these two are nothing else, they at least possess the virtues of being frank and earnest!

One of the most memorable sequences I clipped many years ago has Frank confessing his sins. He says: "All my sins were sins of omission; I could never get organized!"

How we use our time is of ultimate consequence to the effectiveness of our lives. In no case is that more true than for pastors. Few vocations offer the amount of flexibility of schedule and personal discretion which pastors can exercise in the use of time. Yet paradoxically, few vocations have the same unusual demands for time with which pastors must cope. It is not a 9-to-5, Monday-to-Friday job.

Most of us (pastors and all others included here) believe that our time problems come to us because of interruptions, which we cannot control. For pastors, of course, such interruptions must always be seen as opportunities for ministry.

The incessant phone calls, the unexpected visit can often begin with "a moment of your time" and extend to an hour! But what an opportunity for meaningful encounter between pastor and member.

Pastors who play the "I'm so busy with God's work so please don't interrupt me" game will discover in the end that there isn't much of God's work to do. The same goes for pastors who rigidly control their time commitments and fail to respond to urgent needs in the congregation.

Alec Mackenzie in a recent book, *Time for Success,* challenges the popular assumption that our time problems grow out of interruptions or sources external to our choosing. The real problem is within ourselves.

Machenzie identifies the following internal and personal reasons why people have problems finding sufficient time to meet either their own goals or the expectations of others. These time barriers include: trying to do too much, personal disorganization, inability to say "no," lack of self-discipline, procrastination, indecision, leaving tasks unfinished, and socializing.

In the same vein, Steven R. Covey in his book, *The Seven Habits of Highly Effective People,* says the real challenge is not to manage time but to manage ourselves.

Persons who learn to manage themselves become efficient and effective in their use of time. They have learned to identify urgent matters which must be responded to if they are important.

But more significantly, they will create the times and spaces in their lives for things that are important though not urgent. It is here that the truly significant contributions of their lives are made as they work at planning, building relationships, creating new opportunities, working toward long-term goals geared toward the prevention of problems, and recreation.

Above all, they have learned to say "no" to those things which are neither urgent nor important because they have a bigger "yes" burning inside of themselves. They do get organized and respond appropriately to the tasks of ministry.

May 3, 1990

30. Ministry Is Rooted in Spirituality

Despite my misgivings about spirituality in the past, I have come more and more to believe that authentic ministry must be rooted in a true spirituality of every pastor.

Spirituality is a big word today. It used to be that humility prevented us from speaking about or claiming too much piety. It was considered an evidence of spiritual pride to talk about one's religious practices. It used to be that the only people who talked about spirituality were those few extra-pious folk whose talk about their religious experience was tolerated at best by most people, even in the church.

No more. Spirituality is now big in almost all religious circles, both evangelical and liberal. Protestants are now journeying to Roman Catholics for spiritual direction, and claiming what they find there with enthusiasm and joy. You cannot walk around our seminaries these days without hearing students and our prospective pastors talk about the importance of spiritual disciplines.

I suppose the spirituality of pastors has long been assumed as a given for who they are and what they represent. It was an obligation of their vocation. While others may not have been particularly pious, in pastors it was not only accepted but expected.

However, I confess that I have not always been impressed by the assumed spirituality of people whose talk is often filled with what seem to be pious clichés. And I am still less than certain that the more contemporary forms of spirituality are taking us to any new or more profound relationships with God or with each other.

Nevertheless, I found myself attracted to the recent book by Ben Campbell Johnson, *Pastoral Spirituality: A Focus for Ministry*, published by The Westminster Press. Seldom have I both argued with and applauded the writings of an author in a single book as I did this one.

Despite my misgivings about religious piety, I have come more and more to believe that authentic ministry must be rooted in a true spirituality. Who we are at the core of our being as persons, "in touch with" ourselves, other persons, our congregations, our world, and with God is what makes all the difference for effectiveness in life and in ministry. Spirituality defined as "in touch with" elevates the conversation to new levels of authenticity and profundity.

Johnson helps me to grasp what such "being in touch" might mean when he writes: "Spirituality arises from the desire and the ability to notice what is happening, to be present to oneself and one's world, and to respond to these data as a person of faith."

One chapter I found helpful was where Johnson described seven types of spirituality, suggesting that various persons might find more meaning in one than another. We should not presume to impose our own preferences on others.

These seven types of spirituality are: evangelical, charismatic, sacramental, activist, academic, ascetic, and Eastern. I found myself classifying the order of these various types of spirituality—from those which have been most meaningful and helpful, to those which have held little or no meaning for me. That process clarified the issue and again helped me to be "in touch with" myself and God.

Reading Johnson prompted me to ponder the times and places in which I have become more aware of the wonder of God's work in my life and in our world. To my own surprise I thought of several experiences of a pilgrimage to a sacred place. These have not always been perceived as a form of spiritual discipline, but I know that they have made a deep spiritual impact upon me.

The most important chapter of Johnson's book is "The Pastor as a Christ-Bearer." Here the issue is not so much spirituality as it is the necessary role which every pastor must embody as the representative of Christ. It is "not a holier or more powerful one, or one of more privilege, but a role as the bearer of Christ, a symbolic presence of God."

Contemporary pastors have had a great deal of trouble in claiming this symbolic role, yet at the heart of the matter of pastoral spirituality is the willingness to accept in a servanthood fashion this essential leadership responsibility.

I found Johnson's book both exciting and disappointing. Read it for yourself. Argue with it. Learn from it. I certainly did both of these.

May 17, 1990

31. Choosing Leaders Without Losers

Churches report that increasingly they are having difficulty gaining the consent of members to run for church office in elections.

Losing hurts. Losing a church election hurts even more. Losing raises questions and doubts about self-worth.

Losing is embarrassing. How can you face others, especially the winners? Losing causes one to wonder whether one has anything to offer the church. Losing inclines one toward withdrawal from active participation.

Despite all this, most of us, myself included, have survived losing in church elections. We have gone on to make other contributions to the Christian community. And eventually we forget, or at least we repress the fact that someone else has been chosen over us.

For all the virtues of a democratic system, and there are many, there are also some liabilities, especially when used in the church. Feelings of rejection remain for a long time.

Let's be clear about one thing: There is nothing in the Bible that says the way to select church leaders is to conduct a democratic election. The Scripture is not clear at all about process. We are told of some persons being chosen, presumably because they had the gifts for leadership and the maturity and wisdom which others recognized.

Churches report that increasingly they are having difficulty gaining the consent of members to run for church office in elections. Just because we have always done it this way does not mean that democratic, competitive elections are the only way for the church to choose persons for leadership. What are the alternatives?

An increasing number of congregations are moving away from elections for office to some form of gift discernment and appointment to office. Let me share how one church is doing that.

The process begins with the church board carefully selecting a small committee to do gift discernment and appointment. These cannot be church board members or pastoral staff. However, they need to be persons who know both the program of the church and the personal qualities of its members.

Ultimately the committee makes appointments to the major commissions or boards of the church, including those who serve as deacons/elders. But before they do that they must ask themselves several questions.

Who has the gifts for leadership? Who will bring vision and energy to the tasks which need to be done? Who are new members of our congregations who could bring new perspectives and ideas?

Who has not been given the opportunity to serve before but might grow with new responsibilities? How can we affirm persons by offering them the opportunity to serve Christ and the church?

Growing churches do not choose only the old-timers for leadership roles. They aggressively invite new persons to service. This means they will look for a variety of ages to be represented. Both women and men will be asked to share major responsibilities.

It is helpful if this committee has access to more information than just their collective memory about those who have served in the past. With computers today, churches can have on record all the leadership responsibilities every member has held over the years.

Having identified a slate of persons to serve, this committee then contacts the new appointees to gain their consent. The consent is to serve upon appointment, not to run in an election. There are no losers.

June 7, 1990

32. Confidentiality Is a Pastoral Issue

Pastors must be able to keep confidential that which has been entrusted to them.

Every pastor will at some time learn information that cannot be shared with anyone. To be privy to such information is neither joyful nor easy.

It is a burden to carry that kind of knowledge about someone else. But the ability to hold information in absolute confidentiality is an ethical issue of ministry.

Often such confidential information will come in the context of pastoral counseling. What the counselee is saying to the pastor is: "I'm sharing with you a secret about my life which I cannot carry alone anymore. I share it with you in order that you may carry it with me and that I may be free from the oppressive hold which it has on my life."

Pastors must be able to keep confidential that which has been entrusted to them. Not to keep such information confidential is to invite a massive loss of trust and respect from everyone.

Some persons may appear to enjoy being privileged to the intimate information of the pastor. But if they know that the pastor cannot keep confidences, they will not entrust their lives to the pastor when they need to. The breakdown of confidentiality has a way of mushrooming and almost always results in loss of confidence in the pastor.

But confidentiality in ministry presents several problems that are not easy to resolve. One issue is how much can at least be shared with one's spouse. Because confidential information is a burden, to share it with one's spouse can help lighten the load.

Again, the pastor must take several things into account. First, to give such information to the spouse is to add to the spouse's burdens: Do spouses need or want that?

Furthermore, the spouse may not be able to keep confidential items. In the guise of spirituality, confidential information has been known to be shared as "prayer concerns." I am grateful for a spouse whom I knew would keep absolutely confidential what I shared within the confines of our relationship.

A second issue for pastors is discerning the fine line between items calling for strict confidentiality and those items which can and need to be shared for reasons of caregiving within the congregation. Some things need to be shared with the deacon/elder group; other things need to be shared with the whole congregation. It is not easy to sort out what is appropriate public information and what is not.

A pastoral counselor recently reported the following: "A physician spoke to me recently expressing concern about the amount and kind of information his pastor gives from the pulpit about hospitalized parishioners. From a physician's point of view, it was a continuous and serious breach of confidentiality.

"No physician would dare share publicly the kind of information that some pastors share from the pulpit about persons who are ill. It is both illegal and a breach of confidentiality . . . . It is appropriate to share with the congregation the fact that a person is hospitalized. Any other details beyond that should be shared only with the consent and/or request of the patient or family."

Finally, the pastor carries the burden of knowing what is both a legal and moral responsibility in situations involving physical and/or sexual violence. Confidentiality here is not an ultimate value under which pastors can hide. Consulting with a trusted professional physician or mental health worker ought to be essential in such cases.

June 21, 1990

33. A Lay Mentor Can Help the Pastor

When Victor showed up at the office, I knew I could count on about two hours of conversation.

I never knew when Victor might show up at my church office, but most often it was a weekday afternoon. Most of the time he had no particular agenda that brought him to the church. He simply came to talk.

No one designated him as the counselor to this young pastor. In fact, most of the church would have been unaware of how often he came or how often he called.

If Victor came without an agenda, he always had something to talk about. We talked about science (his field) and theology (my field). We talked about politics, both as it related to government and as it related to the church.

Living in a major metropolitan area as both of us did, I remember Victor once talking about farm organizations. There was hardly a field of human endeavor about which he was not knowledgeable, though I don't recall that we ever talked about sports!

When Victor showed up at the office, I knew I could count on about two hours of conversation. Whatever was to have occupied my time that day would be set aside. I confess that sometimes I resented that. In retrospect, I know that it was always time well spent.

Most persons who come to the church office to see the pastor do so because of their needs. I would like to believe that in some way Victor's visits did something beneficial for him. But mostly he came for my needs: my needs for perspective, for alternative opinions, to see a larger world, and my needs as a beginning pastor for nurture and support.

Victor came from that generation that knew the Bible. He

could pull out the most appropriate verse or phrase and relate it to some contemporary issue. Or sometimes a phrase would be shared which was like a window to the world—a fresh perspective from which to view reality. His knowledge of the Bible never ceased to amaze and challenge me.

What Victor was for me in that first pastorate I would wish for every pastor. He was a lay mentor to the pastor. He was someone who helped me look at faith and congregational life and the mission of the church with eyes and ears that were different from and more experienced than mine. And sometimes I'm sure his counsel prevented me from being my own worst enemy as a pastor. I'm grateful.

Recently I had some conversation with another lay member in another congregation. Like Victor, he, too, cares about pastors and about congregations. He, too, is knowledgeable about many things and has broad involvements in concerns of both church and world.

This person shared his joys about the apparent good beginning of the new pastor in his congregation. He told about how the pastor was open to his counsel as well as his friendship. And then he told about how a previous pastor had been unreceptive and had not listened to him or other members of the congregation.

Being a mentor to the pastor is not for everyone, and sometimes those self-appointed persons do not bring wisdom, love, or insight. But I am convinced that almost every congregation has persons whose counsel and friendship could prove valuable to every pastor.

One of my deepest regrets is turning down an offer of regular counsel from another wise member in my second congregation—because I thought I was already too busy. I was the loser.

August 2, 1990

34. Pastor's Pay Is a Matter of Perspective

Pastors will look at the facts one way; those who represent congregations will look at the same facts another way.

Being both fair and honest around issues dealing with pastoral salaries is not easy. Perceptions get distorted; facts get twisted; and feelings get hurt.

My number-one rule about pastoral salaries is that everyone adjusts the honest facts in a way that will benefit their perceived reality, which is usually their perceived benefit. Pastors will look at the facts one way; those who represent congregations will look at the same facts another way.

For example, if you ask: "What is the pastor paid?" you can receive four answers—and maybe more. The pastor living in the parsonage will tell you the cash salary and not take into account the value of the parsonage. It may be to the pastor's perceived benefit to appear underpaid compared to others, in the hope of receiving more.

A second answer is that the pastor is paid the cash salary plus a housing allowance, reflecting a salary more comparable to a typical employee in another occupation. Usually when the pastor asks for a cost-of-living adjustment, the pastor expects that this percentage will be applied to this salary figure.

A third answer to the question: "How much is the pastor paid?" is to add to the cash salary and the housing allowance those items which are included in a benefits package. This usually includes a percentage for retirement investment, some form of medical coverage usually including the family, and some provision for continuing education.

This increases the amount that the pastor receives by several thousand dollars and thus gives a quite different answer to our question.

I have learned that these items in the benefit package, particularly health insurance (in the United States), are included in the annual cost-of-living adjustment of most professions as well as in the manner by which this national cost-of-living figure is arrived at.

When the cost-of-living adjustment is applied to only the pastor's cash salary and the benefits are added above that, then the pastor has received a substantial bonus, which may of course be well justified. But we ought to know what we are doing.

A fourth answer to the question usually comes from the point of view of the church that wants to look at the "bottom line." This is to really answer the question: "What does it cost the church to have a pastor?"

To answer that question one must add to the cash salary, the housing allowance, and the benefit packet the reimbursements for professional expenses. Typically this has meant some form of auto allowance for miles driven as a part of doing the church's job. And sometimes conference expenses are appropriately figured here.

This fourth part, reimbursements, really are not part of the pastor's salary, of course. And therefore they should not be included to answer the question: "How much is the pastor paid?" But since this section can add several additional thousand dollars to the church budget, one can understand why the typical church member might think it should be included in what it costs to have a pastor in this congregation.

How one treats all of the facts is significantly determined by which side of the experience you sit on. To deal as honestly and openly about all the facts as possible is to the long term benefit of all. Both pastors and those who represent congregations need to be helped to see how it looks from the other side.

September 6, 1990

35. Church, Not Pastor, Owns "Office"

The office of ministry belongs not to the clergy or those who have been ordained. Rather it belongs to the church.

An important but neglected aspect of ministerial leadership is vested in what has traditionally been called the office of ministry.

In the United States we sometimes speak about the office of the presidency, meaning a position within our nation that is greater than the individual who occupies that office at any given time. It is a position of respect and responsibility which was there before the present occupant and will be there after the current president completes his term. The respect for the office may be enhanced or diminished by the way the current president fulfills that responsibility.

The office gives the occupant certain privileges, but it also carries unique and added expectations. Furthermore, persons who occupy that office are called upon to be accountable for the way they carry out their role and responsibilities.

Similar things are associated with the office of ministry in the church. But first we ought to ask: To whom does the office of ministry belong?

It is natural and common to answer that question by saying that the office of ministry belongs to the pastor. After all, she or he has been ordained into that office. It seems logical that it therefore belongs to the pastor. Logical perhaps, but theologically wrong!

The office of ministry belongs not to the clergy or those who have been ordained. Rather it belongs to the church, even as the office of the presidency belongs not to its occupant but to the nation.

How can I say that strong enough other than by repeating it? The office of ministry is the church's office. If those who occupy that office abuse the privilege or fail to serve the church, the church can reclaim it from them.

In effect, the church loans out the privilege of occupying its office of ministry. It belongs to the minister only in the sense of being granted, for a time, the stewardship of how that office is filled. Furthermore, it is the minister's only as long as that person continues to earn the trust by which it was given.

The office of ministry is greater than and more enduring than the gifts of the persons who assume its privileges and its responsibilities for a time. The whole is certainly greater than the sum of its parts.

What privileges and rights does the church give to those who occupy its office? Among other things are the following: (1) an established position from which to speak to and for the church in a way not given to everyone, (2) the right to enter without specific invitation into personal and family situations calling for pastoral care, (3) access to information and other forms of power, (4) access to groups and decision-making bodies with whom leadership is shared, (5) the privilege of leadership of the whole body, and (6) the right to declare the Word of God as the pastor understands it; sometimes referred to as the freedom of the pulpit.

What then are the responsibilities and expectations of the one who occupies the church's office of ministry? (1) An obligation to proclaim, interpret, and defend the Christian gospel, (2) a commitment to love and care for the church, even when one is critical of it, (3) a duty to represent the church when its symbolic presence is needed, particularly in pastoral care, (4) an obligation to act ethically and without partiality in all relationships, (5) a willingness to fulfill the tasks expected by the church to the best of one's abilities to do so, and (6) a readiness as the servant of Christ and the church to act sacrificially and without need for acclaim when duty demands it.

Finally, the office of ministry calls for the person who occupies it to submit to both supervision and accountability. This will include at least the following areas: (1) for one's credentials; (2)

for the manner in which one works and serves within the church; (3) for continuing growth as a pastoral person; (4) for living an example of high moral standards; and (5) for the exercise of stewardship of body, mind, and spirit.

October 4, 1990

36. Seek First to Understand Others

If the congregation senses that the pastor loves and cares about them, they will take seriously what the pastor preaches, even when they disagree.

I thought I was paying careful attention. Certainly I had no trouble understanding what the person was saying, and I believed that I was hearing accurately the all-important messages between the lines.

"Do you hear what I am trying to tell you?" the person asked, either implying that I was not sufficiently intelligent to understand or he was incapable of saying what he really meant. To prove the point, the person repeated the story, concluding again: "Do you hear what I'm trying to tell you?"

By that point, of course, I heard more than he thought he was telling me. I heard a person who was both insistent and confident that he knew the truth. His very insistence on making himself and his point of view understood had planted a seed of doubt in my mind. Perhaps there was another side to the story. I had better find out!

I recently was involved briefly in a congregation which has been experiencing considerable conflict within itself. As I listened to people, it became quite clear that everyone's highest purpose was to make certain that they were understood and that their point of view would be heard. And sometimes that is essential.

But before any significant progress can be made toward reconciliation, the perspective must be changed. Stephen Covey put it this way in his book *The Seven Habits of Highly Effective People:* "If I were to summarize in one sentence the single most important principle I have learned in the field of interpersonal relations, it would be this: Seek first to understand, then to be understood."

This principle is rooted in Scripture, and therefore we should have known it all along. "Let each of you look not only to your own interests, but to the interests of others." (Phil. 2:4).

When it comes to persons in leadership responsibilities in the church, this principle is especially pertinent. Take pastors for instance. Pastors who operate as though their primary goal is for the congregation to understand them and their point of view will almost inevitably find themselves running into resistance and suspicion.

On the other hand, pastors who approach their ministry with the mind and heart to listen, to learn, to first of all understand those to whom and with whom they would minister, will discover willing, cooperative, and supporting workers in the church.

But how easy it is to get it wrong, saying to ourselves quietly if not verbally to others: "Do you hear what I'm trying to tell you?" I have reported many times on a study that was done about Lutheran pastors and their attitudes and relationships. The conclusion goes like this: If the congregation senses that the pastor loves and cares about them, they will take seriously what the pastor preaches, even when they disagree.

If, on the other hand, they do not experience this love and

care, and do not sense that they are being understood, they will doubt that the pastor is preaching the Word of God!

There are several ways to describe the person who puts into practice the principle: "Seek first to understand, then to be understood." They make themselves vulnerable. They identify with others and understand their experiences and perceptions. They are teachable. They listen, listen, listen.

They understand the meaning of Covey, who wrote: "To touch the soul of another human being is to walk on holy ground."

November 1, 1990

37. Widows, Widowers: Include Them

"Religion that is pure and undefiled before God, the Father, is this: to care for orphans and widows in their distress." (James 1:27).

"More empty promises are made at funerals than anywhere else." Those words burned their way into my soul. They were the words of a widow from one of our strong and good congregations.

We are familiar with the promises to which she referred. In all likelihood we have made such promises ourselves. "If there is anything we can do in the next months, we'll be more than happy to help you." "You won't be alone; we'll be there to be with you." "We want you to be part of our family; you'll be included." "We love you and we'll remember you."

What is the reality? What happens after the funeral? What do both widows and widowers experience? As I hear the story and from what I observe, the promises and the reality do not match.

Oh yes, there is an initial time or two in which we make some effort to stay in touch. But then . . . nothing . . . no one. Or at least so it seems.

As a pastor I had an ideal for follow-up pastoral care after a funeral. It was to visit the surviving family member in four days, again in four weeks, and again in four months. I know that even as pastor I almost never followed my own ideal. It is so easy to forget and to get busy with other things. Isn't it?

We hear a lot about God's special compassion for the poor and the oppressed, usually meaning the economically, socially, and politically deprived. What we have too often forgotten is that alongside of that is the clear biblical statement of God's special care and compassion for the widow and the orphan.

"Religion that is pure and undefiled before God, the Father, is this: to care for orphans and widows in their distress." (James 1:27). When Jesus looked for an example of generosity and good stewardship, he found the poor widow with her two small copper coins.

One of the needs uncovered in the early church was the result of a complaint: "The Hellenists complained against the Hebrews because their widows were being neglected in the daily distribution of food." (Acts 6:1). Though the text is not explicit, tradition has often interpreted this event as the origin of the deacons, those whose task it is to care for persons with special needs.

What is interesting in this passage is that the complaint is in behalf of widows, presumably all women. When the church responded to this need, they assigned the responsibility to seven men! One of the modern complaints I hear from widows is the almost total loss of contact with males, as though suddenly half of the world has ceased to exist.

What most persons who live alone long for, whether they be widows or widowers or other singles, is to be included in a diversity of social situations with men and women, couples and singles, family and friends. What better place to begin than in church?

In the setting where the comment was made about the empty promises at funerals, I heard additional stories. They had to do with waiting for the pastor who never comes. They had to do with coming to church on Sunday morning, meeting several couples and then being left standing alone while the couples went into the sanctuary to sit together. She went home!

The worst and at the same time most hopeful story came from a widow who told how she had taken the initiative, even at some risk. It had become custom in that church to set a table in the corner where the widows could all eat together. She refused.

Instead she found her brother and his wife, and asked if she could sit with them. "Why, of course," they said. But why did she have to take the initiative?

November 15, 1990

38. Is Pastoral Care Being Neglected?

What marvelous opportunities to be agents of God's grace to persons in times of crisis.

Three things are required and expected of every pastor: the first is public ministry. Usually we think of this in terms of preaching, leading worship, teaching, and leading groups.

The second is person-to-person ministry. This includes every one-on-one contact between the pastor and members of the congregation. This includes various forms of visitation, counseling, and all informal points of meeting in face-to-face relationships.

The last is administration ministry. This has to do with the structured and organizational life of the community as the pastor enables the community of the church to function effectively.

All three aspects are essential; none are optional. That is not to say that every pastor will do each of these to perfection. We all have greater strengths in some areas than others.

As basically an introvert, I always had to work much harder to do at least the minimum in the person-to-person ministry; it did not come naturally. It was always easier for me to find "important work" to be done in the office.

Evidently the same could be said about other pastors, at least from reports which have been coming my direction recently. I am dismayed, dare I say appalled, by recent reports I have been hearing about pastoral failure in person-to-person ministry or what we more often and more appropriately call pastoral care.

When I talk about failure here, I am not talking about those who don't visit in the homes of all the members once a year, nor about those who don't make the rounds of the nursing homes at least once a month. I never achieved those goals either.

The failures I'm hearing about are failures to visit critically ill persons in the hospital, failures to respond to family members who've experienced significant emotional trauma, failure to respond immediately at times of death or other major catastrophe.

What is going on? Why do some pastors apparently believe it is no longer essential to respond to situations calling for pastoral care and pastoral presence? Have they missed something in their training and preparation for ministry? What is their assumption about the nature of the pastoral tasks?

Our theology of ministry has played down the symbolic role of the pastor in the life of the congregation. Pastors want to be prophets, but apparently they don't want to be priests.

To carry out a priestly role in ministry is to represent something more than yourself. It is to be a representative of the congregation and, even in the eyes of some, a representative of God. "How can we do that?" pastors ask.

Perhaps some pastors rationalize like this: If we believe in the priesthood of all believers, why should I be expected to represent either the congregation or God? Why shouldn't other members respond to crisis needs just as much and as soon as me?

Without in any way denying the valued insight of the priesthood of all believers, it is urgent that we recover an understanding of the uniqueness of the representational and priestly role of pastors.

What marvelous opportunities to be agents of God's grace to persons in particular times of crisis. What wonderful chances to come near to members of the congregation in person-to-person relationships which will strengthen their faith in God and in their pastor.

Pastors must not miss these opportunities. When someone is in the hospital, go. When the house burns down, be there. When an accident happens, respond now. When someone dies, leave what you are doing and go. It is both your opportunity and your duty.

February 7, 1991

39. The Interim Doesn't Just Fill Time

It is an important time for congregations to set new directions and to develop new patterns of relationships. It is definitely not wasted time delaying something better yet to come.

I recently received the following letter: "Dear John: We are debating the merits of having an interim pastor. Would you have any helpful information of the pros and cons of using an interim pastor?

"We seem to have some strong feelings within our congregation that we should get an interim to help us through the grieving process as our pastor leaves. Others have strong feelings that we are already going through the grieving process since we have known for so long that our pastor will be leaving.

"An interim pastor would only cause two disruptions instead of one. Any information that you could share would be much appreciated. Sincerely, Kathryn."

Dear Kathryn: I'm glad you asked about the interim pastor for your congregation. It is easy to understand why congregations perceive the interim or transition pastor as an unnecessary and extra delay in finding permanent pastoral leadership. However, the issues are much more complex than simply grieving the loss of a well-loved pastor.

The interim pastor has traditionally been seen as a person who fills time in that gap between the leaving of the former pastor and the coming of the next pastor. We want to make certain that there is someone to fill the pulpit during this time and to take care of at least the essentials of pastoral care in cases of illness or death in the congregation.

While it is often good to have some time between two pastors which might be filled by someone in this interim role, there are three situations that call for something much more intentional than filling time.

Generally a transition pastor is essential in any congregation in which there has been major conflict within the congregation or between the congregation and the former pastor. The second situation which calls for interim pastoral leadership is where the pastor has had a long tenure and has been highly appreciated. And finally if there has been a traumatic event in the life of the congregation, an interim/transition pastor is almost essential.

Congregations seem most to need this transitional leadership in opposite situations, one negative and the other positive. In both of these cases the task of this interim pastor is much more than to fill time or to fill the pulpit.

The accepted wisdom is that if congregations do not find an intentional interim pastor, the next pastor will become, in fact, the interim and will stay only a short time.

Pastors are not carbon copies of each other. Each one has unique gifts for ministry. Pastors have different priorities. Pastors have different personalities. When congregations have grown accustomed to one style of ministry over many years, it is not easy to accept something different and new.

Congregations also have high expectations, sometimes too high. They want the new pastor not only to do well what the previous pastor did well; they also want the new pastor to do perfectly what the former pastor did poorly.

Transition pastors can help congregations become more realistic about the common humanity which pastors and congregations share.

In cases where there have been significant congregational conflicts, we are learning how much a skilled transition pastor can work to bring healing and wholeness, leading a congregation into a more positive and hopeful future.

You will notice that I have been using the words interim pastor and transition pastor almost synonymously. The word interim tends to suggest just filling in the time or the gaps. I tend to use the word transition pastor more because it communicates that it is a time with a specific purpose and goal.

It is an important time for congregations to set new directions and to develop new patterns of relationships. It is definitely not wasted time, delaying something better yet to come.

Thank you for asking about this critical moment in the life of your congregation. Given the long and good experience which you have had with the present pastor, I would hope you might prepare for a continuing positive future by considering having a transition pastor between. Sincerely, John.

March 21, 1991

40. You Need to Grow If You Minister

It is one of the obligations and privileges of all pastors that they commit themselves to a lifetime of spiritual, intellectual, and relational growth.

If this were a sermon (and perhaps it is), my text would be from 2 Peter 3:18: "But grow in the grace and knowledge of our Lord and Savior, Jesus Christ."

It is one of the obligations and privileges of all pastors that they commit themselves to a lifetime of spiritual, intellectual and relational growth.

Why is continuing education so important for pastors? First

of all, one simply cannot share with others in preaching and teaching what one has not first learned oneself. Pastors who think they can minister for a lifetime off of what they learned in college and seminary are kidding no one but themselves.

Furthermore, our world is constantly changing, and people in the church are normally growing persons. The educational level is constantly rising in our society and therefore within the church. Pastors who would remain in touch with their congregations must grow with those to whom they would minister.

But there is an even more important reason than either of the above, and this relates to the scripture text of 2 Peter. Those who would serve Christ and his church are empowered for their ministry by their own growth in grace and knowledge. Peter is talking in this text about something far more important than increasing intellectual understanding, essential though that is.

He is pointing toward the fact that spiritual growth must happen in the depths of the heart and soul of every pastor. There must be growth in self-understanding, but with that must be growth in understanding the ways of God.

Can pastors plan for and program such growth? No, not exactly, but we can place ourselves in settings where such growth experiences are most likely to happen.

A multitude of workshops and seminars are available these days. There are continuing education programs at many seminaries. There are opportunities for spiritual retreats. There are graduate degree programs such as the popular Doctor of Ministry.

Pilgrimages are possible to places important to your spiritual heritage or to the places of our Judeo-Christian origins in Israel, the West Bank, and the entire Mediterranean area. There are opportunities for growth in the various programs of supervised and clinical pastoral education.

And then there are always books. Books hold the treasure of new ideas, new experiences, new perceptions, new interpretations. Books are the basic and essential tool of pastoral growth.

To facilitate these many forms of personal and professional growth for pastors, our congregations have the privilege and responsibility to assist in providing the time and financial resources to make some of these growth opportunities possible.

Most congregations today include in their annual budget an amount to use only for such continuing education programs. To participate in such programs, pastors must have time available away from their regular responsibilities. Sometimes funds are also available from area conferences.

Stephen R. Covey identifies continuing personal and professional growth as the seventh habit of highly effective people. It is the key to both private and public victory, enabling one to experience more fully God's grace and to gain that knowledge of Christ which is essential to all who would serve in the kingdom of our Lord.

April 4, 1991

41. When Things Aren't Quite Right

People today have relatively little tolerance for annoyances, particularly in church.

When I was a boy, it seemed I always got things that weren't quite right.

First came my bicycle. World War II had just ended, and bicycles were hard to get. As I remember, you put your name on a waiting list. Well, the local bicycle shop tried to beat the system. Some people got genuine Schwinns.

But me? The shop ordered all the parts of a bicycle and put it together. That's what I got, and it always peddled harder than the Schwinns my friends and cousins had.

My electric train would never go fast enough to run off the track like other boys' trains, so what fun was that? My sled was stiff and you couldn't steer it. The pockets on my carom board* weren't deep enough, and so the caroms bounced back out.

My music stand had only one extension rather than two, so I could only sit to play my cornet—which wasn't the trumpet that I wanted. You get the picture, don't you?

Remembering these childhood experiences helps me understand why I am something of a perfectionist today. Now I want things to be right. When I shop for something, I am less concerned with price than with whether I will be happy with my purchase in the long run.

Recently we attended a concert in our church. The music was good and sometimes wonderful. I came home singing to myself.

But sitting in the balcony was not good. In fact, it's another of those things that wasn't done right.

As the story has come down, it wasn't the architect's fault, either. When the church was under construction, someone decided that two rows could be added to the front of the balcony, so why not?

Thirty-five years of frustration have told us why not. The only people who can see what's going on are in those first two rows. For the rest of the balcony, forget it. Listen, but don't try to participate visually.

The reason we ended up in the balcony was because the church was full. We weren't late. In fact we were at least 15 minutes early. That provided an opportunity to view the frustration of dozens of others who came to join us in the balcony.

---

*a kind of billiard game

Group after group came in, looked for seating possibilities, took their chosen seats, looked around for other options which might give a better view, got up and moved to another location in the slight hope that it might be better.

No sooner had they moved than another family or group did the same thing, not once or twice but literally dozens of times. Some left the balcony for who knows where.

Those who stayed did one of three things: (1) they sat on the top of the bench back; (2) they got up and down throughout the concert so that by standing they could see a few people performing for parts of the concert; or (3) they resigned themselves to their fate and resolved to come earlier next time to avoid the balcony.

I think I came through my childhood frustrations with things that weren't quite right without resentments or other negative reactions. But people today have relatively little tolerance for such annoyances, particularly in church. Doing things right the first time can help lead to long-term satisfaction.

April 18, 1991

42. Must the Pastor Go to Every Meeting?

Others can bring wisdom and creativity to the work of the church, but they will only do so when the pastor is not always present.

Several years ago I was told about a church where some of the committees and boards began to plan their meetings in such a way that the pastor could no longer attend every single committee meeting. This occurred in a highly successful congregation where the pastor was a well-loved and much appreciated leader.

But hidden behind this action was more than a hint that the pastor was over-functioning and too controlling by his persistent presence. The church and those members in leadership responsibilities needed some spaces in their thinking and action outside the shadow of the pastor.

This was not one of those congregations where the pastor is systematically denied a leadership role, which is another issue needing to be addressed sometime. But in a typical congregation which expects much from its pastor, it illustrates the delicate balance in leadership responsibilities which every congregation and every pastor want and need.

So pastors face a dilemma. If they attend every committee and board meeting, they are thought to be too controlling. If they fail to be present at times when committees look for the potential wisdom and resources the pastor might give, they risk being thought of as uninterested, uncaring or even irresponsible.

This raises the larger question about the pastor's leadership role. Is the pastor simply a functionary expected to do only certain tasks such as preaching and visiting the sick? Or does the pastor have a more central role of leadership to guide and enable the congregation to fulfill its vision?

I have a strong bias in favor of the latter option, one in

which the pastor is a central figure who stands in the middle of the congregation's life and work. It is a role not to dominate and control but to lend vision, to help coordinate and to enable and empower the whole congregation for its ministry and service.

But does that mean the pastor must attend every committee meeting in order to do this? I don't think so.

Certainly the pastor should be expected to attend the primary leadership bodies of the church: the council or board, the deacons or the elders. But beyond that, discretion is needed. Perhaps occasional or selective attendance is enough to give support and direction to the work of commissions and committees.

It is also possible for the pastor to keep in touch either by phone or meeting with the committee chairperson. Learning to delegate responsibility to others is also a key element in leadership.

Sometimes the congregation is most empowered by learning not to depend only upon the wisdom and insight of the pastor. Others can bring wisdom and creativity to the work of the church, but they will only do so when the pastor is not always present.

This calls for trust. The pastor must learn to trust others. The congregation must learn to trust the pastor.

It also calls for communication, which incidentally helps to build trust. Being physically absent does not mean being left out of the circle of communication. Trust grows as pastors sometimes learn to depend upon others.

Isn't it amazing that God depends upon us to establish his church!? As Jesus prayed in John 17:11: "And now I am no longer in the world, but they are in the world, and I am coming to you. Holy Father, protect them in your name."

The work of our Lord is being carried on, even though he is not physically present at every board and committee meeting.

May 16, 1991

43. Communion's Element of Surprise

When I remember this Savior, I'll take the real bread, crust and all.

Several stories about communion services contain elements of surprise and humor. God must sometimes laugh with us and at us in our attempts to be serious and pious.

And if God can laugh (as the psalmist reports that God does), then we can laugh occasionally about our human foibles in our most religious moments.

We have learned to partake of the communion elements in various ways in the last several decades, knowing that new meanings and insights can happen when we are open to something other than the routine.

One of the ways that we have learned to share the bread is by passing a piece of bread for each person to break off a smaller piece for either themselves or their neighbor.

I will not forget the time when the piece of bread was passed down the row with the expectation that each one would partake. It so happened however, that the first person in the first row had no one to observe how this was to be done. It had not occurred to me that I needed to give explicit instructions.

So when the bread was given to him, he did what comes naturally. He took the bread and put it to his mouth, took a bite and passed it on! Was that "common bread"?

Then there is the great story about the missionary pastor who knew how to be flexible and innovative when the situation called for it. Neither wine nor grape juice evidently were available, so what is the closest thing to it?

How about warm grape Jell-O? It's only a symbol, after all, and God would understand the intent. Missionaries have always learned how to adapt, so it was grape Jell-O for the cup.

Well, you've already guessed it: The Jell-O cooled and the Jell-O hardened. And when the congregation went to drink, nothing came out. Somehow I think God must have enjoyed that communion service more than many of our sincere pretensions to serious piety.

Well, I really do have a few serious comments about the elements we use in communion. I know it really doesn't matter to God, who first of all looks on the heart of each one of us as participants. That is first and foremost. The symbols we use are secondary.

But I have never understood why we use the little cubes of white bread. And why cut off the crust?

This bread represents the broken body of our Lord, and something about that suggests to me that it would be a stronger symbol if the bread were of the whole kernel of wheat, crushed and ground together. That is real food for people who need something of substance.

And why not retain the crust? God comes to us, not in pretty little symbols of perfection without spot or blemish, but with one whose body is bruised and broken.

Or as the prophet Isaiah says: "He had no form or majesty that we should look at him, nothing in his appearance that we should desire him . . . . But he was wounded for our transgressions . . . and by his bruises we are healed" (Isaiah 53:2, 5).

When I remember this Savior, I'll take the real bread, crust and all.

The same goes for the cup. I have been in several congregations of our denomination, usually in Canada, where wine has been served at the Lord's table, an authentic reminder of the bitterness of death and a reminder of the wine received by Jesus on the cross just before his words: "It is finished." (John 19:28-30).

At the opposite extreme was the time in our congregation when sweetened frozen grape juice was used, to which must have been added an extra can of water. Weak, insipid, and lifeless. The symbol carried no power in itself to suggest the passion and life-giving love with which our Lord gave his life for the salvation of the world.

Let the symbol of the fruit of the vine be robust and full-bodied, unsweetened and undiluted so that we might partake of the fullness of Christ's grace.

June 6, 1991

44. Pastors Have Missionary Duties

The church now lives in a post-Christian or non-Christian culture. Ministry today must reengage itself with the missionary task, serving the institutional needs of the congregation and the missionary needs of the world.

One of the most popular authors writing about congregational life and pastoral leadership today is Kennon L. Callahan. A former professor at Perkins Theological Seminary and now a church consultant, Callahan is engaged in developing his images of effective congregations and effective pastors.

"The day of the missionary pastor has come," Callahan asserts in his book, *Effective Church Leadership*. Callahan's thesis is that the professional pastor used to serve a church which assumed the culture about it was Christian. He says that is no longer true. The church now lives in a post-Christian and non-Christian culture—a theme currently in vogue, as reflected in a book titled *Resident Aliens* by Hauerwas and Willimon. Those of us who represent the radical reformation could have told these authors all along that we have never and do not now live and minister in a Christian culture.

I can also enthusiastically agree that we need today a new awareness of and commitment to the missionary task of ministry by all pastors. By this Callahan means more than a pastor who supports missions. He means the pastor perceives himself or herself as a missionary, responsible for proclaiming and interpreting the Christian message in a non-Christian world.

Callahan also offers considerable wisdom and insight into the nature of leadership, especially as it relates to pastors. In his critique of the concept of the pastor as enabler he writes: "In actual practice, many enablers are not really enablers; they are covert manipulators. They use the techniques of process, coupled with a pseudo-pastoral psychology, to manipulate the group toward an already self-ordained conclusion."

He suggests that much of our current forms of pastoral evaluation are responsible for the low morale of pastors. Again I agree.

"I am amazed at the charity and goodwill of pastors. They sense that the top-down process (of evaluation) reinforces passive-aggressive behavior, advances a sense of low-grade hostility, deepens subliminal resentment, and increases the likelihood of eruptive forms of anger. It is a wonder pastors handle the results as well as they do."

As all books, this one by Callahan needs to be read with a critical mind, ready to embrace insight and truth while discarding that which is not helpful. I found Callahan's style rather wooden and repetitive at times. I felt his definition of the professional pastor was negative and unfortunate. I also am uncomfortable with his "either-or" thesis that pastors can choose to serve the institutional needs of the congregation or the missionary needs of the world. Both must be held near to the center of every pastor who would be an effective church leader.

Nevertheless, I want to embrace his driving passion—that ministry today must reengage itself with the missionary task.

July 18, 1991

45. Forbidden Sex a Betrayal of Trust

When a relationship in this forbidden zone becomes sexual, everything that had been good about the relationship is lost.

The evidence continues to accumulate that sexuality has become a substantial problem in the church. I say this without even considering the divisive debates around abortion and homosexuality.

What troubles me are the continuing accounts of pastors and others in the service of the church who are accused of crossing the boundary of legitimate sexual relationships.

Some months ago a trusted colleague recommended that I read the book by Peter Rutter, *Sex in the Forbidden Zone.* At the time I thought I had read enough on the subject and ignored his suggestion. But dealing with yet another case of pastoral indiscretion prompted me to order and read this book. I'm glad I did.

Well, let's face it: Reading about other people's sins, especially sexual sins, is itself quite stimulating. It is also incidentally depressing. But neither of these are why all clergy should read this book.

Peter Rutter is a psychiatrist in San Francisco and chairman of the ethics committee of the C.G. Jung Institute. The book has no explicit Christian or even religious orientation, yet the values which underlie his work are those which Christians would gladly embrace. Central among these are concern for the well-being of the other person.

His central thesis is that sexual activity involving men in power—therapists, doctors, clergy, teachers, and others—always involves a betrayal of the victim's trust. Furthermore, it is psychologically damaging, even when it is claimed and perceived otherwise.

Rutter describes the woundedness which all persons bring to

every relationship, whether male or female. It is in the hope of healing and fulfillment that we find each other and offer to one another the care and compassion that makes us vulnerable.

He describes the unique role which sexual fantasy plays in the life of every male. Like the forbidden fruit of the garden of Eden, the fantasy seems to promise healing. Instead it yields only confusion and destruction when the fantasy is acted upon and becomes reality.

Citing numerous examples including clergy, when a relationship in this forbidden zone becomes sexual, everything that had been good about the relationship is lost. Almost the inevitable result is a loss of respect, a loss of relationship, and often the loss of one's vocation for violating the ethical boundary.

So how do we guard the boundaries of the forbidden zone? In separate chapters for women and men, Rutter makes helpful suggestions for each.

"Know the wrongness of sexual abuse of trust," he writes to the men. "No matter how tempted you may feel by the magical lure of forbidden sexuality, nothing makes it right—not even the woman's willingness to have a sexual relationship, not even her outright seduction."

Does that mean that men and women must live isolated lives with no interaction outside the bonds of marriage? No, Rutter describes the goodness which can be experienced between men and women relating to and working with each other—when they have given up the sexual agenda between them.

This is a book for all in ministry today, knowing the unique temptations they face in the forbidden zone. But it is also a book for all, including lay people, who seek greater understanding of themselves.

September 19, 1991

46. "Ex Officio" Duties Misunderstood

The pastor may exercise influence but should honor the checks and balances which limit the decision-making role to other members of the church.

One of the most common phrases used when talking about church organizations and bylaws is the Latin phrase *ex officio*. And almost always it is used incorrectly.

What we think it means is someone we invite or expect to participate in a committee or board of the church but who is not actually a member of that committee or board. And we often assume in addition that such a person who is *ex officio* has no vote or final role in decision making. All we expect is that person's presence and wise counsel.

Thus it is quite common for congregations to identify the pastor as an *ex officio* member of all boards and committees of the church, thus granting him or her the right to attend any meetings.

Given the above assumptions, such a provision is both well-intentioned and wise. The pastor should have this kind of access to the church's organizational life.

There is only one problem. This understanding of *ex officio* is not the correct interpretation of the term, according to *Robert's Rules of Order*.

Unless explicitly stated that *ex officio* members have no votes, they must be considered full voting members of every committee or board. They can make motions and fully participate in the decision-making process like every other member.

What does *ex officio* mean? Literally it means "out of the office." For a pastor to be an *ex officio* member of a board or committee, it means that he or she is automatically a member by virtue of being in the office of pastor. And of course, when the person ceases to be pastor, he or she also automatically ceases being an *ex officio* member of all boards and committees.

The position of *ex officio* is by no means limited to the role of the pastor. For instance, it might be that the chair of the deacons or elders could be designated an *ex officio* member of the church board or council. In such a position the deacon or elder chair would be a full voting member of the board or council.

Another idea which might have merit would be to make the conference minister or overseer an *ex officio* member of the church board or council, or of the deacon or elder board. This is possible even if that person is not a member of the congregation.

The conference minister or overseer clearly has a significant interest in the welfare of the congregation and its future, and should be given access to places of significant decision-making responsibilities. Though having the full rights of a member of that body, such an *ex officio* member is not counted as a part of the quorum.

The question still remains whether it is wise to make the pastor an *ex officio* member of boards and committees in the church. I believe the pastor already has such power and influence in the congregation that is it neither necessary nor wise for the pastor to be *ex officio* in other boards and committees.

I do believe that the pastor should have the right to attend all meetings, but without vote or the power to make motions. The pastor is called upon to exercise his or her influence through the powers of persuasion, but also to honor the checks and balances which limit the decision-making role to other members of the church.

To do this it may be helpful to designate the pastor as *ex officio* in boards and committees. But I would always be careful to designate that this is without vote.

November 17, 1991

47. When the Christmas Candles Fizzle

Normally I am quite competent to perform candle surgery alone. But the sizzling-candle mystery called for assistance.

It's not quite like the awesome experience of those shepherds on the hills outside of Bethlehem. But each Advent brings an observant eye from the congregation as children of the church come forward to light the Advent candles.

Everyone is watching . . . and wondering: "Will the candles light this year? Will they stay lit?"

Candles are a wonderful symbol of Christmas, the celebration of light and life which comes to us and to all the world in the birth of Jesus Christ.

Candles invite our thoughtful meditation about things beyond our mundane lives. They speak to us of that which is mystical and transcendent. Candles bespeak the quiet flames of spiritual passion which burn within us.

Despite all the warm feelings which candles give us, they are fickle and sometimes almost unmanageable, failing to do what we want them to do. And never is this more true than the candles of the Advent wreath, which mark the four Sundays of the Advent season.

Knowing that candles sometimes vary in quality, we determined that we would go to a candle shop to purchase the large candles for the Advent wreath. There would be no embarrassment this year of candles that would go out. Or at least that was our hope.

It was to no avail. In fact, it was worse than ever. It used to be that candles would slowly dim and finally self-extinguish.

But this year was different. The candle would light and burn for a time. Then there would be a sizzle . . . and out they would go!

This called for action. Nothing in seminary training for pastors prepares one for occasions such as this. But experience had taught me that one of the required tasks of pastors was to be a candle surgeon. A handy pocket knife was all that was required.

Normally I was quite competent to perform candle surgery alone. But the sizzling-candle mystery called for surgical assistance from my wife. Bernice is appropriately a nurse and employed on the surgical floor of the local hospital. Needless to say, her training had not prepared her for this task, either.

After a few cuts and stabs to the sick candle, Bernice took the candle in hand and began to shake it. Low and behold, what to our wondering eyes should appear . . . but drops of water! What was water doing inside this Advent candle? It came from the candle store, not the discount store, remember?

I suppose there must be a moral to this pastor's Christmas candle story, but I've chosen to not even think about what it might be.

In contrast to our Advent candle that year is the account of Saint John, who interprets the true meaning of the incarnation in the poetry of his prologue to the gospel. He puts it like this: "What has come into being in him was life, and the life was the light of all people. The light shines in the darkness, and the darkness did not overcome it."

The true light of Jesus Christ still shines brightly in our dark world—despite our flickering foibles and Advent candles with water in them. May Christ's light shine brightly for you.

December 19, 1991

48. Four Ways to Decide About Pastors

Pastors, like all of us, need to feel that they are more than pawns being manipulated and controlled by others.

Who decides whether a pastor is called to your congregation? Who determines when it is time to end that relationship? And how are these decisions made?

I have identified four basic systems churches use for these important decisions. These systems might be called (1) theocracy, (2) bureaucracy, (3) democracy, and (4) monarchy. Let me describe each of these and how they function for us.

Theocracy: The basic meaning here is that God rules and therefore, God decides. This has been done by using the lot, after the example of the early church in Acts 1:26. I have heard the lot referred to as a "holy process." Since God makes no mistakes, the person is called to that ministry position for life.

The use of the lot has a long history in parts of the Amish and Mennonite churches. At its best it communicates with more clarity than any other process that God is at the heart of this decision.

Persons are called to ministry not out of their own ambitions nor because of their pride in the position of leadership which they hold. They are there simply and only because God has called them.

Bureaucracy: Many Christian churches have discovered that there is value in the wisdom of the larger church and of those who see things at a different perspective from the local setting.

This has generally meant that the bishop and those who assist the bishop are ultimately responsible for decisions of pastoral placement These churches function with a true placement system rather than a calling system. It is most typical today in the United Methodist Church.

A pastor is appointed to a congregation and serves there until the bishop decides a change is needed. The advantage in this system is that changes can be made more quickly to benefit the larger church and the individual congregations. It can help to avoid major pastor-congregational conflicts and involuntary terminations.

Democracy: This system puts the focus of the decision on pastoral tenure directly on the congregation. The people being served decide whether a pastor comes or goes. Most often this is done by a congregational vote. But other means of discernment could also be used. It describes those churches that are most congregational in their polity, such as most Baptists.

The effect of this process of calling and terminating a pastor is to make it a highly political process. Those being served must give the pastor their approval or disapproval.

But at its best, this method preserves the integrity of the role and power of the congregation in giving their consent and affirmation. Leadership is not forced upon them. They have had an authentic role in choosing who is to serve as pastor, and for how long.

Monarchy: The final possibility is that the decision regarding pastoral tenure is made by the pastor, either with or without consultation. The important point here is that the pastor has power not only to affect the congregation, but most important, has the ability to decide on her or his own life. This would often be reflected among independent churches, where the pastor exercises extra-ordinary power.

Viewed positively, pastors, like all of us, need to feel that they are more than pawns being manipulated and controlled by others. They have the responsibility to be attuned to the Spirit of God and the will of the congregation, but ultimately the decision is theirs.

They may choose to stay in the congregation as long as it seems good, or until a better opportunity comes along ("God is calling me to this new challenge"), or until a conflict may cause too much pain.

Each of these methods maintain essential understandings. But even more significant is that each of them on its own is inadequate and has proven unacceptable. Many denominations have tried to combine these elements in some kind of balance including Presbyterians, Lutherans, and even Episcopalians. Today this balance is also being sought among United Methodists, Mennonites, and Baptists.

As we look for reforms of our polity, we must seek authentic ways to involve all four options in making decisions about pastoral tenure.

January 16, 1992

49. Pastors Formed by Many Factors

The seminary's cultural environment is often the most powerful form of learning in a future pastor's spiritual formation.

I was recently part of a conversation at Associated Mennonite Biblical Seminary, discussing possible changes in the seminary curriculum.

The assumption underlying this discussion is that the future pastor will be formed by the courses of study taken during these years of graduate education. It is an assumption with which I agree, but only in part.

Pastors, like all other human beings, are formed out of an incredibly complex set of experiences and relationships. The quality of our pastors and those who would be pastors is affected by several identifiable issues, only one of which is the specific courses of study taken during the years of education. Can we identify some of these factors?

The most fundamental issue takes us directly to the person of the pastor. Who is this person, and what does she or he bring to the challenging and difficult task of ministry?

It has to do with intellectual competence, but even more to do with perceptual skills. It has to do with spiritual and psychological health. It has to do with attitudes toward life, self, others, God, learning, the church, and a whole range of relationships.

Here we talk about issues of identity, authenticity, empathy or the ability to enter into the feelings of others. Here we look into the "being" of the person, the internal self, or what the Bible speaks about as the heart and soul of each of us. Experience tells us that education does relatively little to change the most basic person we are. This is the given with which we must all begin.

A second reality is that pastors, again as all other human beings, are formed out of the models of and relationships with other persons.

Today we are becoming keenly aware of the important formation experiences which come from mentoring. We learn what pastors ought to be and do by observing and identifying with those who are already pastors.

Teachers are also key role models for would-be pastors, not simply for what they teach but out of who they are and the relationships they establish. Almost all of us could point to the powerful role which a teacher had in shaping our life and work, whether in ministry or any other vocation.

The psychologist Heinz Kohut calls this element in the formation of the self "merging." By strongly identifying with someone or something greater than oneself, values are formed and would-be pastors come into being. Should seminary faculty be hired as much with this in mind as for their academic contributions?

Pastors are also formed out of the prevailing expectations of ministers both in the church and in the world. Cultural images of what a pastor is can be significant in both positive and negative ways. Consider the image of ministers in the media and the popular culture of our society; it's not very encouraging.

Congregational expectations and individual members' demands affect our sense of what a pastor ought to be. The church's prevailing theology of ministry has a pervasive and often unchallenged effect on the understanding of who the pastor is and the role the pastor eventually assumes.

Finally, the schools and seminaries which our would-be pastor attends are significant in the shaping of pastors. Here the curriculum is important. It does make a difference what one studies and learns in this disciplined setting of education.

The church expects pastors who love and know the Scriptures and can "rightly handle the word of truth." The church needs pastors who understand the issues of theology and who know the history of the faith lived out in the church over many centuries.

The church today demands pastors who are skilled in the "arts of ministry" and who can relate to others with the gifts of pastoral care. Yes, curriculum is important.

But almost as important in the seminary context is what I would call the culture of the seminary. This is what gets communicated indirectly and outside the classroom.

It has to do with attitudes, prevailing assumptions about life, faith, and the church. It's what students learn from each other as much as it is in what they learn from the faculty. It's what happens in the worship experiences within the chapel as much as what happens in the library.

This cultural environment of the seminary is often the most powerful form of learning in a future pastor's spiritual formation.

March 5, 1992

50. Ushers Give the First Impressions

With a positive spirit and welcoming smile, ushers can do a lot to help set the tone for people as they come to worship.

I had a unique opportunity recently to usher on Sunday morning in our congregation. We have several usher groups who take turns, and this year a new group was formed to usher on the fifth Sunday of the month when that occurs. The new group is made up of the ordained members who are not pastors.

Our congregation has an excess of such persons due to our location and the church-related institutions in our community. So why not put us to work in this important role?

I once heard the suggestion that ushers are really the "face" of the congregation. If they are the persons who give first impressions as new persons enter, then that may well be true.

Ushering is something most people can do, but that does not make it an easy or simple task. I determined that I would be somewhat assertive to encourage people to sit toward the front by asking them: "May I take you to the front?"

I was surprised how many were ready to do that with my suggestion. Others specified more clearly where they wanted to be. Still others had a mind of their own. Ushers have to be on the watch for those who choose to seat themselves along the way.

Ushers can do a lot to help set the tone for people as they come to worship. A positive spirit and a welcoming smile can help everyone say with the psalmist: "I was glad when they said to me, 'Let us go to the house of the Lord!'"

A second responsibility of the usher in most congregations is to assist in receiving the offering. That too is an interesting experience for the inexperienced like myself. Yes, we did start the offering plates down one row from both ends!

Customs differ. In most congregations the offering is taken front to back, but I have been in several in which the offering is taken back to front. I don't imagine there is any significance except habit, though it has always seemed helpful to be able to anticipate by seeing the usher coming toward you rather than surprising you from behind.

Since this ushering crew of ordained persons was new to the task, we were given a sheet of instructions and gentle reminders, which included the following: "Arrive in plenty of time. Smile, be courteous, and friendly. Be alert to people's special needs, such as wheelchairs. When in doubt, act confident, walk briskly, don't run. Do not chew gum.

"Do not cheat yourself of the opportunity to worship. If you are aware of your duties and perform them properly, you will be able to worship with the congregation of which you are a part."

I'm glad for the opportunity to usher and thus to understand more clearly this valuable service given weekly in our churches. Perhaps it has something to do with the scriptural insight: "I would rather be a doorkeeper in the house of my God than live in the tents of wickedness."

April 16, 1992

51. Understanding the Meaning of Symbols

Sometimes we have responded to symbols with a dulled imagination, having eyes which don't see and ears which don't hear.

Many of us have a hard time understanding symbols. Sometimes we have seen them as objects of inappropriate worship, participating in the idolatry forbidden in the second commandment.

Sometimes we have viewed them with the narrowness of a literal interpretation, mistaking the object for the reality to which it points. And sometimes we have responded with a dulled imagination, having eyes which don't see and ears which don't hear.

Nevertheless, symbols are all around us. Symbols are a part of every culture. Every act, every object, every word participates in the symbolic richness of life. Even people can assume symbolic roles.

The Bible is full of symbols, especially in words. The Gospel of John is constructed around a wealth of images: creation, light, water, doors, shepherds, and sheep, among many others.

How then can we come to more positively understand the meaning of symbols, and especially of artistic and religious symbols? Test the following suggestions for the truth they contain.

1. Symbols bear within them a representational quality. The cross, for instance, represents not only two pieces of wood and some nails. It represents the Lord who suffered and died on that cross. Often the cross is used to represent the incarnation, including the life and teaching, as well as the death and resurrection of our Lord.

2. The symbol participates in the reality which it represents, yet it can and must be differentiated from that reality. The

lighted candle participates in the light of God's presence among us, but we always must know that the lighted candle is not God.

3. The symbol condenses a larger reality to a human scale so that we can begin to comprehend the incomprehensible. The globe speaks to us of a world too large for us to see, yet a reality which we experience every day.

4. The symbol makes available to human experience that which transcends the ordinary, certainly that which transcends the rational and scientific. Yet it is perceived as truth with meaning. It is often diminished by the rational, though it is not irrational.

Indeed, the symbol often participates in paradox. A church building cannot contain God, yet it can become a place where God's presence is known and thus becomes for us "Bethel," the house of God.

5. The symbol is always communal and thus can be shared with others. While it is experienced in personal ways, it must also be available to be experienced by other persons with eyes, ears, and minds to see, hear, and comprehend.

Thus baptism is not a private act but a highly personal event which occurs within the context of the community, whose members are not only observers but also participants.

6. The symbol is material and incarnational. Symbols have a physical quality that can be seen and touched.

Even the symbolic act must have something substantial which the senses can perceive. To eat of the bread and to drink from the cup of communion is to taste and see that the Lord is good and gracious.

7. The symbol lends insight or adds meaning into our experience at a level of height and depth beyond the merely trivial. To engage ourselves in the symbolic act of worship is to know both God and ourselves more fully, and thus to live more faithfully as disciples of Christ.

8. The symbol has no meaning in itself. It is therefore highly dependent upon the meanings we ascribe to it.

We can choose not to give meaning to the symbols about us.

But that does not diminish the power of the symbol. Instead, it greatly diminishes the richness of our own lives.

May 21, 1992

52. Where Do Pastors Find Support?

Pastors need to bare their souls to someone. They need someone outside the congregation with whom to test ideas, hopes, and dreams.

"One of the things I want to have is a support group when I enter ministry." "Every pastor needs a support system." "Where do you find support in your congregation?"

Support is the key word. It is regularly voiced in ministerial circles today as an expectation and as an essential to survival in ministry.

What we are less clear about is where and from whom the pastor can gain this support so essential to survival in congregational leadership. And what is expected?

I agree that some forms of personal and professional support are essential for pastors. But I am not ready to agree with every expectation I hear voiced about how and where to find that support system.

Support often comes from the experiences of shared leadership with various members of the congregation. Good relationships grow out of shared vision and energy put to work in the variety of congregational programs.

Thus a pastor might find significant support in the work of ministry from working with the elders or deacons. Or for some this supporting working relationship might be found in the chair of the Outreach Commission. There are many possibilities.

Another key group to which pastors may look for support is a special group assigned to look after the pastor-congregation relationship. This group is to be a bridge of communication to maintain the best of good working relationships. They are responsible for keeping the memo of understanding up to date, and recommending salary changes each year or planning for a major evaluation process.

Is this a support group for the pastor? Usually, yes; but not always. Or at least not in the ways that pastors often expect.

What pastors want and legitimately need is some resource to whom they can bare their souls. They need persons with whom they can be very honest and who will be honest with them. They need someone outside the congregation with whom to test ideas and hopes and dreams. They need someone who can respond and interact in helpful ways that are mutually nourishing.

My experience is that such relationships are seldom found within the structures of the congregation within which one ministers. And even less often are the quality of relationships found within formal structures assigned to meet this need.

That means pastors themselves must be responsible for finding and cultivating the relationships that will be the kind of support that will carry them forward in ministry. Don't expect the church or someone else to do it for you.

Often such persons turn out to be colleagues in ministry, persons with whom one shares a common vocation but who are sufficiently outside one's own congregation to be objective. Sometimes they may be from other denominational groups. Sometimes they can be enlarged to becoming family friends so that the pastor's spouse also benefits from the relationship.

Could the pastor's spouse be part of such a support system? Why of course, though this, too, will vary among clergy couples. One must be careful not to put expectations into the relationship which one's partner cannot or chooses not to carry.

I find myself reaching out in many directions for the variety of support needs I experience. I look for relationships of mutuality so that I contribute as much as I benefit. I look for persons whom I perceive to be nourishing rather than depleting my limited spiritual and emotional energies. The old-fashioned word for such persons is friends.

June 18, 1992

53. Planning Makes All the Difference

I found that I functioned best if I had basic sermon themes planned ahead anywhere from three to six months in advance.

This is about congregational and pastoral planning. By that I mean planning for the life, program, and activities of a congregation.

Almost everything involves planning. We really have few spontaneous experiences. That may be why we enjoy them so much when they do occur. Planning is often hard, if not tedious work.

What is the planning cycle in your congregation? Is it week-to-week, monthly, annually? What events actually need more time than a year of planning if they are to occur? I recently met with a pastoral staff of one congregation that was moving into planning two to three years in advance.

Who does what planning? What are the specific pastoral responsibilities when it comes to planning? If it is a multiple-staff congregation, how do staff members work together for effective planning? What events call for planning with other leadership groups in the church?

Most of us have never thought that the issues were quite that complex and involved. But that is probably because someone has done effective planning behind the scenes.

As a pastor, one of the most important tasks is to plan ahead for preaching. I found that I functioned best if I had basic sermon themes planned ahead anywhere from three to six months in advance. Not only did sermon preparation become much easier, but I could then draw upon readings which might relate to sermons weeks ahead.

I was invited by a small rural congregation to be the fall Bible study speaker two years in advance. I confess that I found it easier to say "yes" when the event seemed so far into the future. And then I learned that this congregation always did it that way. Wise planning!

Other special events such as major congregational anniversaries may require more than one year of planning if they are to be carried forward effectively.

Leadership planning retreats can be a helpful way to do shared planning. Our multiple-staff group met annually in one of our homes with brunch to plan a year-long basic schedule.

Other planning retreats involved leadership from the boards and commissions to think ahead about our common life in the congregation. These were sometimes held at campgrounds over a weekend. Such retreats served several purposes in addition to planning.

They helped us to learn to know and experience one another

in more intimate ways, and to build trust. They also allowed us to think beyond the planning of programs to the setting of longer-term goals. Eating and sleeping together in a camp or retreat setting builds relationships in ways not otherwise possible.

July 2, 1992

54. Tamed Cynic Affirms the Pastoral Ministry

Where, other than the ministry, can one invest one's life where it can be made more effective in as many directions?

This is not your latest best seller. In fact, the original copyright is from 1929, eight years before I was born. So why would Harper and Row continue to publish this book about ministry when most books about ministry came yesterday and are gone tomorrow?

The answer is in the reading. It is deservedly a classic by a person we do not normally associate with ministry, but with theology: Reinhold Niebuhr. I'm sorry it took me so long to discover *Leaves from the Notebook of a Tamed Cynic*.

I read the book somewhat after the manner in which it was written. It is a journal account which this young pastor of the Bethel Evangelical Church in Detroit wrote occasionally throughout his 13 years as pastor of that congregation.

In such a manner I read the book over an extended time, digesting several entries in the journal and then laying it aside perhaps for weeks between.

In his preface and apology, we are introduced to the heart of a pastor who understands both the joys and the temptations which ministry holds.

"Having both entered and left the parish ministry against my inclinations, I pay my tribute to the calling, firm in the conviction that it offers greater opportunities for both moral adventure and social usefulness than any other calling, if it is entered with open eyes and a consciousness of the hazards to virtue which lurk in it.

"I make no apology for being critical of what I love. No one wants a love which is based upon illusions, and there is no reason why we should not love a profession and yet be critical of it."

There are gems of wisdom throughout the book:

- "They say a young preacher must catch his second wind before he can really preach. I'd better catch it pretty soon or the weekly sermon will become a terrible chore."
- "I am really beginning to like the ministry."
- "One who has lost his illusions about mankind and retains his illusions about himself is insufferable."
- "I am sorry that the sense of awe and reverence has departed from many of our churches."
- "There is at the heart of almost every tradition an element of reasonableness and around its circumference a whole series of irrationalities."
- "Faithful church attendance develops and reveals the virtue of patience much more than the virtue of courage."
- "I learn how to be tolerant when I become the victim of somebody else's spiritual pride."

Niebuhr is critical of many things: inconsequential preaching, pastors who compromise their integrity, arrogant intellectuals, industrial and economic injustice, etc. This critical spirit is tolerable because Niebuhr is also critical of himself. It is as

120

though he can step outside of himself and honestly observe the inconsistencies of his own life and faith.

In his final year as pastor, 1928, Niebuhr reflected on the 13 years of ministry and wrote: "Granted all the weaknesses of the church and the limitations of the ministry as a profession, where can one invest one's life where it can be made more effective in as many directions? Here is a task which requires the knowledge of a social scientist and the insight and imagination of a poet, the executive talents of a businessman and the mental discipline of a philosopher."

And it is still an enormous challenge and a rewarding vocation.

August 6, 1992

55. How Should the Church Raise Funds?

Major gifts have a distorting effect. Congregations that receive such gifts are wise to disperse them to larger causes.

Most Christians believe we have both the privilege and responsibility to offer to God and to the church our financial support. It is one way of participating in mission and of extending our commitments beyond the boundaries of our immediate influence. At its highest, giving is a form of prayer.

A debate is going on in the church, however, about appropriate methods of fund raising. In general the issue is posed as follows: Should the funds necessary to support the institutions of the church be raised in and through congregations or through direct person-to-person solicitation? To most people, that may not sound like an issue to fight about. But it does generate considerable emotion and discussion among institutional leaders.

The present consensus is that the answer to this question is to be found in a theology of stewardship. So our fund raisers and theologians are being linked in the debate. They are being called upon to help the church find a solution or at least some answer that will justify our efforts to raise the needed contributions to sustain our institutions.

May I be so bold as to suggest a simple answer? It is not particularly biblical or theological, but I think it makes practical sense: Give from income primarily through the congregation. Give from accumulated capital through those persons and institutions who have earned your trust and confidence.

Most of our giving comes from one of two sources: (1) The financial share which we give from our weekly, monthly or even annual income. The key factor is that it has its origin in a percentage of our income. (2) Financial resources which some persons give from accumulated capital. These are resources which may have been saved from earlier years of income or accumulated through business or investments.

Church institutions depend on both sources of financial support. Especially schools and retirement communities, hospitals and retreat centers, and increasingly denominational programs must have the financial support which comes from accumulated capital to survive.

So how does this help to solve the debate as to who and how financial support should be solicited? Those of us whose primary source of giving is from our regular income naturally give primarily through our congregations. Congregations thrive when their support comes from the routine giving of every member. It reflects the most immediate sense of loyalty and commitment.

Congregations can also be the agents of the larger church programs and institutions. Those of us who give from income can share in the total work to which the church commits itself for the sake of Christ's kingdom.

On the other hand, congregations do not thrive and often wither when they are the recipients of giving from accumulated capital, especially if it comes to them in the form of an endowment. Major gifts have a distorting effect on congregations. Congregations that receive such gifts are wise to disperse them to larger causes.

When church institutions that depend on gifts from accumulated capital seek to challenge some members to give, they must do so discreetly and in ways that do not do harm to congregations. This normally means some form of individual or person-to-person contact is needed.

Those with accumulated capital to share do so as a result of the trust which they have placed in another person and the institution or cause that person represents.

They generally have the wisdom to know that they can best support both their congregation and the larger church by giving to each appropriately and in ways that do not cause dependency.

September 3, 1992

56. Pastors: Keys to Church Growth

The quality of pastoral leadership is the single most important factor in the life, health, and growth of the congregation.

There was a day when we didn't think about church growth. It happened naturally through the birth of children to existing members. And so the church passed from one generation to another. It wasn't quite that simple, but almost. That day is almost gone.

Every congregation that hopes to grow in numbers and in faithful witness to the gospel must be clear and intentional in its purpose. Church growth has become a growth industry with volumes of books, multitudes of workshops and seminars, and denominationally-sponsored programs.

With that in mind, I confess that it is rather presumptuous on my part to think that I can say anything new or even worthwhile in a few words. Nevertheless, I'll try.

W hat are the essential factors in healthy, growing congregations? I would look for:

1. The spirit or tone of the congregation. Every congregation, like every person, has a sense of self, which is made up from attitudes, beliefs, and behaviors. Growing congregations have a good sense of collective self-esteem.

The members' attitudes are positive and optimistic. There is a sense of confidence about the future, and an awareness that good things happen here. People perceive that they are spiritually nourished by their participation in the congregation, both in what they receive and in what they give. God is present.

Related to this tone of the congregation is a clarity of identity. They know who they are and what they value. They are clear about relationships and loyalties. They are intentional about growth, involving everyone in that inviting, welcoming spirit.

2. The congregation's program. Congregations do things, and they do them together. What they do we call the program of the congregation—that collective set of activities which we also call congregational life. A key component of most people's expectations today is quality. Are things done well? Is the time I give to the church a quality investment of my time and energy? Is what we do meeting real or only imagined needs and expectations?

That may sound like the program is what the church does for people rather than with people. The reality is that a good program has a participatory factor today. There is opportunity to be involved. Leadership is open, and new persons quickly feel themselves to be part of the inner circle.

3. Pastoral leadership. Pastors will argue with this. They will deny the centrality of their role in the life and growth of the congregation. But congregations know intuitively that it is true. The quality of pastoral leadership is the single most important factor in the life, health, and growth of the congregation.

Pastors set the tone. They become the central defining symbol of what this congregation represents. They serve in a representative role in behalf of the whole congregation.

When it comes to church growth, it will not happen if there is not some level of commitment to that from the pastor. And by commitment, I don't mean wishful thinking. I mean energy, desire, and hard work.

The pastor is a key factor in whether or not the congregation has the potential for growth. Let's not hide behind excuses or theological rationalizations which are self-serving. The quality of pastoral leadership is highly determinative for who and what our congregations are becoming.

September 17, 1992

57. Churches Driven by Competition

Our contemporary market-driven religion is forcing us to ask questions of quality and service. We could do worse when we contemplate church growth.

I wish it weren't so. My theology about the church tells me it is not the way it should be. But neither my wishes nor my theology will change the reality.

That reality is that the church is being driven today by marketplace competition. Churches grow or decline by the public perceptions of the quality of what they offer. Even our language reflects the dominance of the economic model when we speak about "shopping for a church home."

It has almost become a truism that there is little denominational loyalty in North American Christendom. Like looking for the best supermarket in the community, people now look for a church that will offer them quality service, good programs as good products, and a friendly environment.

In a word, we look for a church which makes us feel good. And if it can all be had at the lowest possible cost, so much the better.

I would prefer to believe that people would choose a church out of the intense commitment to its beliefs and values. I wish that personal loyalty to one's heritage could be assumed, believing that we owe something to that which has nourished us in our formative years.

I would hope that commitments could be made with an eye toward service to Christ and the church rather than with an eye simply for what one hopes to receive. It all smacks of the "cheap grace" that Dietrich Bonhoeffer so opposed.

Having said all this, I must make a confession. I, too, am a part of what I bemoan. All I need to do to understand how pervasive our market-driven religion has become is to look within myself.

In my work I have opportunity to visit an unusual number of congregations. Too often I have come away telling myself how difficult it would be for me to choose to make that my church home and the location of my faith commitment.

The pettiness of our church conflicts, the dullness of our so-called worship experience, the repetition of sharing times, and the persistent feeling of being the outsider does not make for likely church growth.

Perhaps market-driven religion is the answer. Faced with strong competition, perhaps we will pay more attention to the quality of our common life within the congregation.

Aware that people will choose based upon their perceptions of value, perhaps we will ask more seriously about the nature of our worship and whether or not it yields any sense of connection with transcendent experience.

The surrounding culture has always affected religious faith and practice, so why should we expect our time and place would be an exception?

At least our contemporary market-driven religion is forcing us to ask questions of quality and service. We could do worse when we contemplate church growth.

October 1, 1992

58. How to Set the Right Kind of Goals

Goals should challenge us, but unrealistic goals do nothing to advance the kingdom of God and, ultimately, discredit the church.

I am serving on a goal-setting task force in our congregation. It has not been an easy assignment, and I'm not sure about the outcome of what we are doing.

Don't take me wrong—I believe a congregation should have goals and work to achieve them. It's often how new things are accomplished for God.

Working with this committee has forced me to ponder the nature of goal setting, to ask about what can go wrong, and to define essential factors that make for a successful process.

I think we have somehow allowed ourselves to move into an evaluation mode rather than a goal-setting mode.

Two essential qualities define the difference between evaluation and goal setting: Evaluation looks to the past with an eye cast for perceived weaknesses or negative qualities. Goal setting is oriented to the future with a dominance of optimism and hope.

What we had done or allowed to happen was to use goal setting as the opportunity for people to voice their little complaints and wished-for changes, many of which were strongly contradicted by others.

The wished-for changes felt like they were goals, but in fact they were based upon minor negative evaluations of congregational life. They would do next to nothing to create the congregation we ought to become by our centennial five years hence— the anticipated event which triggered the goal-setting process in the first place.

This experience has helped me identify some factors that ought to be part of any goal-setting process. Do you agree?

1. Goals must be measurable and somewhat tangible. That is not new with me—it's one of the basic rules. Goals and values are not the same thing. Values are essential to good goals, but values are not measurable. One must be able to determine precisely if one has reached a goal—that is what we mean by measurable.

2. Goals ought to be challenging and imaginative. If it is something that would happen anyhow under ordinary circumstances, it is not really a goal. Goals ought to inspire people to new and unexpected levels of achievement.

3. Goals must be attainable and realistic; a polarity to balance No. 2. Great but unrealistic intentions do nothing to advance the kingdom of God, and ultimately they discredit the church and its leadership. Goals, however worthy, which are not attainable do not inspire confidence and faith but contribute to distrust and withdrawal of support.

4. Goals must be related to the identity and mission of the church. They must embody our best values and further our noblest ideals. It is possible to have goals which are popular in the public eye, but which will only serve to undermine who we really are.

5. Finally, goals must be owned by those who will enable them to be fulfilled. That is never easy. What is easy is for some persons to create expectations for others to accomplish, without any real commitment on the part of those whose support is essential.

November 5, 1992

59. The Budget: Good News or Bad?

Positive reinforcement creates positive attitudes. Giving does not decline when the nagging goes away.

About November each year, something approaching the following appears in many church bulletins:

Receipts to date: $75,000

Budget to date: $83,333

Expenses to date: $80,000

Receipts under budget: $8,333

Expenses over receipts: $5,000

What does your faithful church treasurer intend to communicate to the congregation? "Please give more money to support the church. You need to know the facts. And these are the actual facts which reflect our giving as a congregation. Help!"

What does the member of the congregation read while scanning the bulletin during the prelude? "Our church is in financial trouble. Something must be wrong. Maybe it's the pastor. I sure wonder what's wrong."

Treasurers and trustees seem to think that the more the above negative message is given to the congregation, the better are the chances that the congregation will respond positively. But it generally doesn't work. Most of us don't give positive responses to negative messages.

What are the facts? What is the truth? And how might the treasurer communicate both the facts and the truth in a more positive manner?

No congregation gives an equal amount in the offering each month of the year. In our congregation, we discovered that most of us give during the year in a similar way to which we generally spend our resources.

In January we give the least— about 6 percent. From February through October our giving levels out more or less at about 7.5 percent a month. In November we could expect 10 percent, and December brought in 16.5 percent of the annual budget.

There is a more truthful way to report the facts of the congregation's stewardship than the example given at the beginning. And the good news is that it is almost always in a form that is positive, helping the congregation feel good about itself and its overall ministry. How can this be done?

To establish a new basis for reporting, our treasurer went over the record of our giving by the month for the previous five years. He came up with the average amount we could realistically expect at the end of that specific month based on actual experience. That was then used to report the facts of the current giving to the congregation.

We quickly discovered that we were almost never behind in our giving—either we were almost exactly on target or slightly ahead. There is good news to report to the congregation!

Positive reinforcement creates positive attitudes about the church and even about stewardship. What is even better is to discover that giving does not decline when the nagging goes away.

So what might the happy church treasurer put in the church bulletin next November to keep the congregation informed? It might look something like this:

Percentage of budget goal through October: 74 percent

Percentage of budget received through October: 75 percent

Total amount of budget goal through October: $74,000

Total amount received through October: $75,000

November 19, 1992

60. The Difference Between Vision and Goals

As I observe church groups that work to define their vision and their goals, I sense considerable confusion. Vision and goals are two quite different things.

The beginning of a new year offers us the opportunity to ask ourselves again: "Who are we, and where are we going?" We can ask that question very personally, and traditionally it results in New Year's resolutions.

We can also ask the same questions about our congregations or conferences or whatever church institution is important to us: "Who are we as a church, and what is our future?" It is an essential question to those who care about and love the church.

The answer can come in two forms. One answer assumes that our destiny is determined and fixed, and there is nothing we can do to change it. The best that we can do is to understand the answers which someone else or fate has determined.

A second answer assumes that we can determine and even change that future by our intentional choices today. All the contemporary discussion about vision and mission statements, about goals and objectives, is based upon this second answer.

We have it within our power and responsibility to chart the course of the church. We must determine whom we wish to become.

That is followed by asking what we must then do to arrive at that destiny. In its most simple form, that is what vision and mission statements, goals and objectives are about.

However, as I observe church groups that work to define their vision and their goals, I sense considerable confusion. Most often the confusion comes in the failure to carefully differentiate between vision/mission and goals/objectives. They are two quite different things and should not be mixed.

There are several very simple ways to describe this difference. Vision/mission has to do with ends; goals/objectives have to do with the means to achieve those ends. Another way to define and compare is to speak about vision/mission as "being"; in contrast, goals/objectives describe our "doing."

People who write about these things, such as Peter Block in *The Empowered Manager,* also wish to make a distinction between vision and mission. He writes: "Our vision is our deepest expression of what we want." In contrast, "a mission statement is a statement of what business we are in."

Another way to look at all of this is to see the words "vision," "mission," "goals," and "objectives" on a scale moving from the general to the specific, or from the long term to the short term.

Describing our vision/mission is to describe our values, the highest and best of our ideals by which we live, or the ideals which are to be achieved. They are the overarching purposes which form the most noble heart of our life and our faith whether those purposes are personal or related to the institutions we serve. They tell us what it is we are aiming toward over the long term of our lives.

Goals/objectives tell us more about the specific items which we must work at during the present and the immediate time if we are to have a reasonable chance to achieve the vision/mission. In fact, they must be sufficiently specific so that they are measurable, and thus can tell us whether we are making any progress.

To make a final distinction, the difference between the goal and the objective is to view the objective as a sub-goal, designed to help you achieve the goal.

Objectives are the most immediate things to do. They are goals broken down into small enough units so that you can see something very specific and can manage to do it well. While goals/objectives are the means by which we work to achieve more noble ends, we generally recognize that the values implicit in the ends (vision/mission) must be first realized in the means (goals/objectives).

How would one apply this to the church? To pastors?

January 7, 1993

61. Setting, Achieving Pastors' Goals

The test of leadership is not whether the pastor can tell the church what to do. The real test is whether the pastor knows who he or she is as a pastor, and what to do in that role.

Everyone, pastors included, is tempted to define the vision/mission and goals/objectives for someone else. Pastors probably want to do this for the congregation. I have preached sermons with the purpose of telling the congregation what to be and what to do.

The problem with this is that it usually doesn't work. People don't look for someone else to define who they are and how they ought to live. In fact, people resist such unsolicited advice. And it doesn't work any better for preachers than it does for parents!

So where to begin? Begin with yourself. Begin with yourself as a member of the congregation. What are your visions? What is your mission? What are your goals, and what objectives will you start with today?

The same answer holds for the pastor. The place to begin is with yourself. The test of leadership is not whether the pastor can tell the church what to do. The real test is whether the pastor knows who he or she is as a pastor, and what to do in that role.

A significant source of conflict between pastors and congregations occurs when pastors begin by telling the church what it should do. All the while, the pastor is confused about his or her own role and what to do. Define yourself!

How are we to do that? Let's try to imagine what that might mean by working at the sequence of vision/mission and goals/objectives.

We begin with vision. Peter Block says a vision has to do with greatness. In other words, every vision must have within it the commitment to high quality and competence. For the pastor, that means that first and foremost is the vision of being a highly skilled minister and servant of Jesus Christ. The vision begins with a commitment to quality and competence.

How might pastors define their personal mission statement? Mission clarifies our roles and whom we serve. Block says a "mission statement names the game we are going to play." For the pastor this will usually mean claiming a pastoral identity, being dedicated to serving the church and its members.

How does one set appropriate goals to move toward achieving the vision/mission? Protestant pastors expect to be preachers. Of course they know there are many more things to do than just preach. But it remains a central expectation of ministers. Indeed, it is one of the necessary goals pastors claim. So let's focus on it.

What are some steps pastors can take on their way to becoming competent preachers who serve the people of God effectively? Pastors can work on several things:

1. Becoming good students of the Scriptures, able to rightly interpret the word of truth.

2. Becoming careful observers of life and the human condition. Among others things, this means being good listeners before trying to be effective speakers.

3. Reading broadly in both religious and secular literature.

4. Sharpening the skills of creativity, since preaching is best done as an art form.

5. Learning effective speaking skills so that people can listen with understanding and appreciation.

6. Learning to enunciate clearly and to project one's voice so that everyone can hear.

Thus might the pastor use the model of vision/mission and goals/objectives to fulfill at the highest level what God calls us to be and to do.

January 21, 1993

62. Person and Office Give Authority

We have placed all the emphasis on the pastor's person or gifts and none on the pastor's office. It hasn't worked.

Pastors sometimes repeat to each other a lament about how they experience their work: "We are given the responsibility to lead the church, but we are not given the authority to do so." These words reflect frustration and powerlessness. Is that the way it should be? Or how are we to understand pastoral authority?

To help us answer these questions I strongly recommend the book by Jackson W. Carroll, *As One With Authority: Reflective Leadership in Ministry.* If a good book can be defined as one that confirms one's own ideas and prejudices, then I would call this a very good book.

I have told pastors that we need to recover two dimensions of leadership if we are going to find the authority we need to function effectively in ministry. We need to better understand the "person" of the pastor, and we need to recover an appropriate sense of the "office" of ministry.

Over the last 30 years we have placed all the emphasis on the person and the gifts or skills that pastors presumably bring to ministry. It hasn't worked. Something is wrong. Something is missing.

First, we haven't understood the person of the pastor adequately. Our language about gifts has misled us. To speak about gifts for ministry seems on the surface to pick up the New Testament language. But too often our speaking about the gifts for ministry gets confused with whether a person has a few public-speaking skills, or some ability to study theology, or the power to form several strongly held convictions.

All these may be valuable, but they fade quickly compared to more profound questions of character: integrity, self esteem, authenticity, and honesty. So our first task is to grasp the kind of person to whom we will entrust the community's authority to lead.

Jackson Carroll gets it right: "If we have authority as clergy, it's because laity perceive us to be reliable interpreters of the power and purposes of God in the context of contemporary society. And this involves both spirituality and expertise, not one without the other."

Second, we haven't understood the meaning of the pastor's office. The office is the authority given by the church, generally in the act of ordination. This means the minister is given both the responsibility and the power to represent the church and its members. It is the right to act—authority—and the ability to act—power.

These two elements, person and office, must always function together and in a way that each supports the other. Pastors who claim authority simply by virtue of their office and without the re-enforcing power of their personal credibility will always become authoritarian and will loose whatever authority they might have claimed.

On the other hand, pastors who seek to serve using only their gifts for ministry and without the supporting power of the church's office will appear egotistical and ineffective. Again Carroll gets it right: "One need not be a non-directive, *laissez-faire* facilitator—a very wimpish image of ministry—in order to share ministry . . . . Authority of office and personal authority are mutually reinforcing."

So what is the answer to those who claim they have been given responsibility to lead but not the authority to do so? The first task is to earn the authority of leadership by the quality of the character and the person you are. When you have done that, the church will give you the office of leadership and the authority that goes with it.

Usually, that is. But that's a problem for another column.

February 18, 1993

137

63. Preaching: Inspiration, Hard Work

Saying that sermon preparation is difficult and demanding is only another way of saying it is highly rewarding.

Preaching is the one task of pastoral ministry that is most frightening to young pastors. It comes with such regularity. Week after week, the responsibility is relentless.

There is an old saying: "The biblical prophets spoke whenever they were inspired by God to do so, but the pastor is expected to preach every Sunday whether the inspiration comes or not."

God knows, and the congregation knows most of the time, that some sermons come more out of determination than divine inspiration. I've had to prepare sermons like that myself. Sunday's coming!

Over time the wise pastor begins to learn some of the tricks of the trade. The hardest thing in all the world for me was to come to the deadline of sermon preparation time with no idea of subject, content or anything else. God may have created the world out of nothing, but sermons don't come that way.

Long-range planning for sermons is one of the tricks I learned. It helped make sermon preparation more joyful and productive. For me it began with putting onto a calendar the long-term ideas for preaching.

Long-term planning often meant building a series of sermons around larger themes or ideas. Or it might be a series of sermons based upon a particular book of the Bible. Or the sequence of preaching might be related to the Christian year and the common lectionary. At other times there were special denominational emphases to be worked with.

This long-term planning made me think ahead beyond the next Sunday's deadline. Ideas or illustrations might fit better with the sermon scheduled in three weeks and should be held over. Already then I had a head start on that sermon and didn't come to the weekly preparation time with nothing going.

The same goes with reading. Always one is thinking ahead. And as one reads, one picks up ideas for sermons yet to come. It happens sometimes without even trying, which always makes the task easier. When one is alert with long-range sermon planning, one begins to observe everything more carefully.

Preaching ought to be viewed as an art form. Creating a sermon is more than putting together a logical lecture. It demands inspiration—that flash of insight into truth, that moment of emotional energy matched with wisdom, that careful attention to words and their power to convey truth.

The hard work of sermon preparation has mostly to do with the preparation of the preacher, which is why it can be so difficult. It has to do with prayer. It has to do with spiritual energy. It has to do with emotional intensity.

That is not to say that sermon preparation does not also have to do with the forming of ideas and the telling of the story of faith. Content is essential. It matters what we say and whether we say it in clear and comprehensible ways.

Saying that sermon preparation is difficult and demanding is only another way of saying it is highly rewarding. Most preachers would confess they find spiritual energy and renewal for themselves by the disciplines of sermon preparation.

Sermon preparation is a unique form of prayer. It is the most common way pastors pray.

March 18, 1993

64. Churches Face New Legal Issues

Today no pastor or congregation can ignore the legal implications of ministry.

The First Amendment to the U.S. Constitution states: "Congress shall make no law respecting an establishment of religion or prohibiting the free exercise thereof . . . " This has meant a broad and liberal interpretation of religious freedom for people and institutions. For the most part, religious people have been able to practice their faith without interference from the state.*

Thomas Jefferson used the metaphor of "the wall of separation" between church and state to describe the intent of the two clauses of the First Amendment to the U.S. Constitution. In effect, the "No establishment" clause and the "Free exercise" clause have served as walls between which there has existed considerable uncertainty and ambiguity alongside of significant freedoms.

We are experiencing a dramatic change in this relationship between church and state. Each is being affected and changed by the other. Sometimes it is to our mutual good. Often where religious faith and the state come into contact, controversy results.

We recently purchased for our office a 1,000-page volume titled *Pastor, Church and Law* by Richard R. Hammer. Hammer has taught seminary courses on this subject to prospective pastors. Today no pastor or congregation can ignore the legal implications of ministry.

All pastors must understand and comply with the unique legal issues around taxes and social security, even with all its

---

*This column is obviously written from a U.S. context, which is most familiar to me. I would expect the larger issues here to find some parallels in Canada.

contradictions. For instance, in the United States pastors are considered employees of the church for purposes of income tax. But when they figure Social Security taxes they must do so as self-employed.

On the other hand, ministers may exercise the right to an exemption from Social Security provided that on the basis of their religious beliefs they are opposed to acceptance of Social Security benefits. They cannot claim an exemption on the basis of opposition to paying the tax or because they believe that Social Security is a poor investment.

Civil rights legislation and the recent Americans with Disabilities Act are causing us to reconsider the kind of questions that can be asked prospective ministers prior to employment.

Churches are no longer free to ignore these issues, and it is right and good that we too have been called to account.

Issues of age, gender, race, and even health are no longer appropriate or legal on application forms, and we are in the process of making such changes. We recently had a pastor call attention to how a question regarding health is inappropriately being used in preventing his finding of a pastoral position.

New legal issues confronting pastors have to do with clergy malpractice, usually in relation to counseling situations. And of course the issue of sexual abuse is finding its way into the courts.

Minnesota has led the way in requiring the church to check for earlier sexual abuse prior to the employment of a new pastor. A pastor with a record of sexual abuse is required to disclose such before employment. Other states are now following Minnesota's pattern.

Pastors or congregations may purchase malpractice liability insurance to protect from future lawsuits. However, I understand that most of these policies are being written to exclude any obligation to pay for judgments against sexual abuse.

On the other side, churches must also guard against lawsuits for defamation of character. This means that we must be increasingly careful if not cautious about how we deal with references. While this puts limitations upon how the church functions, we are and ought to be committed to dealing with all persons with fairness and justice.

We can only expect the issues of legality between church and state to grow more complex. The day of appealing to the high wall of separation as a justification for our ignorance and doing whatever seemed right in our own eyes is fortunately passed.

Most of us will not become legal experts. But neither can ministers or the church any longer act as if they are beyond the law.

May 6, 1993

65. When Worship Surprises

Some Christians judge the quality of worship by the sermon. We can look for special moments in many parts of worship.

We had an incredible experience in church last Sunday. It came as a surprise in the midst of what appeared to be an ordinary worship service.

The occasion was the special music. The bulletin called for the chancel bell choir together with the clarinet played by John Banman. In the past, flutes have been used with the bell choir with nice effect, so I expected something of the same.

From the first note, we all knew this was something different. The melody was the old gospel hymn, "Just a Closer Walk with Thee," but the musical style was jazz.

Now, I have been around bell choirs and have attended several national bell choir festivals, but never had I heard anything like this! There were sounds and rhythms that I didn't know bells could produce. It was a moment of ecstasy, a feeling or emotion uniquely tied to special experiences of worship. And the congregation responded appropriately, with spontaneous applause. "Clap your hands, all you peoples; shout to God with loud songs of joy. For the Lord, the Most High, is awesome" (Psalm 47:1-2).

Am I suggesting that every congregation ought to have bell choirs that play jazz in order for our worship to be meaningful? Absolutely not. As a matter of fact, our congregation is much more oriented to the Christian classical tradition when it comes to music. I hope and expect it will stay that way.

My point is twofold. First, the elements of surprise and delight are special gifts that ought to come to us occasionally in worship. Such surprises will lift us out of the routine and ordinary experiences, so we must be open to "sing a new song unto the Lord."

Second, we can experience and should look for these special moments in many different parts of our Sunday morning worship. I learned this many years ago from a colleague and friend who understood worship better than I did as a pastor.

She told me how she finds different elements in the worship experience meaningful from week to week. Sometimes it is a hymn of the congregation. Other Sundays it may be a prayer. It may be at least occasionally the sermon.

Some Christians judge the quality of worship by the sermon. If the sermon is good, then worship has been good. If not, then . . . Not so with my friend. She came with a sense of openness to discover God in many different places or through different people or through various worship experiences.

I have been thankful for her wisdom many times when some services in the house of the Lord didn't do much for me. If not in the whole, then look for God in the parts!

What worries me about experiences like we had this last Sunday is the almost inevitable pressure pastors will feel and hear. "Why don't we have something like that every week?" Not only would that destroy the element of surprise, but the new would soon grow old and routine.

You will remember the biblical story of the disciples asking Jesus to institutionalize the transfiguration by building three worship centers on the mountain, following the high and holy moment they had experienced. Jesus refused, understanding the necessity of returning to the valley of service to ordinary people in everyday situations.

Personally, I don't want jazz as my steady musical diet in worship every week. But last Sunday it was just right. And as a result I went on my way singing and believing that our worship had brought us to "just a closer walk with thee."

June 3, 1993

66. You Don't Have to Be Rich to Give

Good planners and managers make good givers. It comes from life choices and being intentional in stewardship decisions.

"Give, even when you have little." Those words came from the voice of experience during a conference I recently attended.

It was the counsel of one who today has achieved considerable financial success, but for whom it was not always so. It grew out of a reflection upon stewardship as a way of living and responding to God's gift of life.

When it comes to money, our powers of rationalization are strong. We tell ourselves we will give when we have achieved financial stability and success. We imagine ourselves giving to the church when there is more than enough and we can give out of our excess.

That day never comes, at least not for most of us. Generosity grows out of the heart and is reflected in an attitude of the soul. It is the conviction that one's life must be connected to that which is greater than oneself, that one has an obligation and a privilege to share in the life-affirming causes of church and community.

Ministers deserve the opportunity to give. Occasionally one hears about a minister who has rationalized that since ministers give so much of their time to the church they don't need to contribute financially. What poverty of the soul! As a matter of fact, the evidence is that pastors are generally among the most financially generous members of their congregations, often ranking near the top in terms of their giving.

Even worse is when congregations think they don't need to pay a good salary to the pastor since the pastor is in the Lord's work. Let the pastor donate part of his or her time, and it won't be taxed! Most pastors would rather receive a fair salary, which assumes they will have the opportunity to make choices about their stewardship and also to experience the joy of giving to others.

A popular stereotype is that pastors are poor financial managers and planners. And of course there are occasional examples of pastors who seem to prove the assumptions correct. Unfortunately, these are often very public, especially when the church is left to pick up the bad debts of a departed pastor.

My friends and colleagues who work with the Mennonite Foundation tell a different story. They say most pastors are responsible and competent in managing their own money.

If that is so, is it because they have learned to give, even when they have little? This suggests there is a link between the generosity of the soul and wise management for a lifetime of stewardship. Good planners and managers make good givers. It comes from life choices and being intentional in stewardship decisions.

My wife and I determined from the beginning of our life together that we would give a tithe of our income, regardless of our needs and circumstances. We did that while we were students. We did that when our first salary was $300 a month, and a third of that went for rent.

I don't agree with the popular theology that suggests God will always financially reward those who give generously. The success-oriented theology of our day flies in the face of a biblical God who is concerned and compassionate for the poor and needy. I never want to forget that.

I also want to always remember Jesus' story of the widow's mite. Generosity is tested not by what we give when we have many possessions and great wealth. It is tested by what we give when we have little.

June 17, 1993

67. Pastors Can Be Homeowners, Too

Our family was part of the move among pastors to provide their own housing, and it was one of the best things we ever did.

Most pastors today firmly believe they should not be treated differently than other members of the congregation.

In a genuine desire to be thought of as one with others rather than one *over* others or even as one *under* others, pastors are asking for ways of being dealt with that are similar to other people.

In former times, with the understanding that pastoral salaries would and perhaps should be lower than their members, pastors often received special discounts from retail merchants.

Fortunately, that day is past. Today pastors are on their own to look for good bargains. There are no longer special deals cut just because one is a minister. The corollary expectation is that pastoral salaries should be in the range of others with comparable education and responsibility.

Housing is a similar issue. Here again, pastors were treated differently than other people with the provision of a parsonage. While other people had to find their own housing and be responsible for its maintenance and taxes, pastors had a home provided with "free rent" and no maintenance responsibilities. Since pastors were not permanent residents, this seemed the reasonable thing to do.

As almost any pastor could tell you, the problem with this arrangement was that it wasn't free rent, and often the arrangement was to the financial advantage of the congregation and the financial disadvantage of the pastor.

This was especially true when pastors took the long-range view of asking where they would live in retirement and how they would have the equity necessary to provide housing at that time.

Homeowners assume the time and energy they put into upkeep and improvement of their property will provide both a more desirable living environment and long-term financial return. As a pastor living in a parsonage, at different times I painted both exterior and interior finishes. We benefitted from having an improved environment, but my labor was a contribution to the value of the church's property.

Sometimes churches are just plain negligent in maintaining the parsonage. When our vacuum cleaner no longer worked because of an old and defective electrical wall socket, the church refused to replace this 85-cent item because the trustee's tester found electrical current in the socket. I soon learned enough about electricity to replace minor items on my own.

Responsibility, self-determination, and value are what home ownership is about. It was not surprising that during the '70s there was a major move among pastors to provide their own housing. Our family was part of that, and it was one of the best things we ever did. Even my relationship with the trustees improved!

There have been other dividends, financial and otherwise. First, it gave us the security that if death or disability should occur, the family could continue to live in our home.

Financially, there were new costs involved. Now we had to assume responsibility for taxes, insurance, maintenance, and utilities, to say nothing of mortgage payments. But there were benefits, as well. Since there have been times of substantial inflation, the value of our home has approximately doubled.

And throughout these years we have benefitted from tax laws that allow clergy both to deduct interest costs and to subtract all housing costs from income for figuring income tax. This benefit is a trade-off for the minister's extra obligation to pay self-employment Social Security tax.

Recently my wife, who is our family accountant, informed me that we were within three years of completing our mortgage payments. That was good news. We will be forever indebted to a leader in the congregation who, 20 years ago, supported us to make the move toward home ownership and was an advocate for us in this decision with the congregation.

August 19, 1993

68. Congregation Can Get It Together

So what is the verbal equivalent of the choir director's hands giving the upbeat signal that will enable everyone to start together on the downbeat?

The little things make a difference in the quality of the experience we have in church. The suggestion I have is a very little thing. Nothing grandiose. No great spiritual insight. In fact, the idea seems almost so small as to be trivial. It will not revive a congregation. It will not bring new vision or a new level of commitment.

So why bother? Does it really matter? It does matter if you feel frustrated, as I do, when the congregation is invited to join collectively in reading, perhaps a Scripture or even a prayer.

When to begin speaking is the question. What is the signal? How does the congregation know when to start? Or are we always supposed to just slide into it?

Typically, the congregation says the Lord's Prayer like this:

". . . in heaven, hallowed be your name . . . ." Or the prayer of St. Francis begins like this: ". . . instrument of your peace. Where there is hatred, let me sow love . . . ."

And the great confession of the church in the Apostles Creed does not begin with the strong credo of "I believe in God . . . ." Instead, the congregation comes sliding in with: " . . . almighty, the maker of heaven and earth . . . ."

So what to do? Many years ago my now deceased friend and colleague Ralph Weber offered me a simple suggestion and solution one Sunday after I undoubtedly had frustrated him with one of the above.

The pastor or whoever is leading the congregation in this public reading needs to think of himself or herself as a choir director. What typically is done is to ask the congregation to start on the downbeat without first giving an upbeat. It doesn't work.

So what is the verbal equivalent of the choir director's hands giving the upbeat signal that will enable everyone to start together on the downbeat? Ralph's idea was for the leader to say: "Reading together . . ."

That's it. It works. People give their minds to the text of the prayer rather than wondering how to slide into this thing without too much awkwardness.

Try it the next time you invite the congregation to join you in repeating the Lord's Prayer, in which case you might adapt by saying for the upbeat signal: "Praying together, (and then the congregation joins), Our Father in heaven, hallowed be your name . . . ."

Little things like this are not going to bring in the kingdom of God. And the issues of justice and righteousness will not be changed by paying attention to such details. But I'm all for removing little annoyances whenever possible.

That reminds me of another: "Shall we pray?" Now that is a good question, and perhaps we ought to ask it more often. But as a signal in worship we never intend it as a question. It is a statement or even a command.

When I was a college student, I remember a faculty member

saying that whenever someone asked in public worship "Shall we pray?" his mind was inclined to respond with a silent "no." It was not that he was against praying, but he was against using the English language to ask a question when a statement of fact was intended.

I confess that to this day whenever I hear "Shall we pray?" my first response is still "no." Perhaps that silent "no"'is itself a prayer that we will all follow the teaching of our Lord to be honest in what we say, whether it be "yes" or "no."

"Let us pray."

October 7, 1993

69. We've Always Done It That Way

Tradition has lost its power to control most things in our world. But if you challenge a church tradition, you can be sure someone will be offended.

"Just ask Thelma; she knows." That is the answer to a question often asked by members of our church choir. The question is: Does the choir wear the gold or red side of the stoles that are part of the choir robes? No one but Thelma seems to know the answer.

So what is the story? I guess Thelma is the only remaining member of the choir who first wore these robes and developed a plan about which color to wear for whatever occasion or season of the Christian year. That was at least 25 years ago and probably longer than that.

What I do know is that throughout the 23 years that I have been a part of this congregation, Thelma is the only one who could answer that question. She has never paused a moment to think about the answer. She always knows. She remembers with absolute clarity the original plan and has singlehandedly made the tradition stick.

By now no one else remembers the decisions or even when they were made. Even more, no one remembers why one Sunday was to be a gold Sunday and another a red Sunday. Tradition has come to mean that "we have always done it this way." And only Thelma knows.

Knowledge and memory are both forms of power. If you knew Thelma you would understand that she does not use her knowledge and her memory to manipulate; she is just passionately committed to the tradition. In her mind, what was decided back 25 to 30 years ago was not only good back then. It was a decision appropriate for all time to come. So Thelma's accurate memory still determines what color to wear when.

Tradition has lost its power to control most things in our world. But in church, traditions can still be strong. Someone with a firm memory can perpetuate a tradition long after anyone else knows why or even cares.

Can you imagine what it would take to change the tradition as entrenched as the one in our church choir? It would take a "gang of white horses" who together determined that they didn't care what was decided 25 years ago. They might want new routines, perhaps to purchase green and white stoles or to wear no stoles. Maybe they wouldn't want to wear robes at all, since they symbolize a high-church concept of the choir. The point is not to debate issues related to choir robes, but to call attention to the place and power which traditions have in our congregations.

Recently a pastor told me that upon coming to serve a large congregation he was told that this decades-old congregation had no traditions. This implied that he had an open playing field in which everything was possible and nothing was assumed.

He soon discovered the congregation had many traditions. He kept bumping into assumptions others made but never shared with him. Traditions were alive and well. They were strong and powerful forces to which he had better pay attention.

Traditions do not have to last forever. Some good traditions do get lost and forgotten. Others should be forgotten or replaced because they no longer hold any meaning. But if you challenge a tradition, you can be certain that someone will be offended.

Pastors should learn to know and appreciate the traditions of a congregation when they begin their ministry there. Skillful pastors also establish new traditions that yield new meanings and memories. And above all, pay attention whenever anyone says: "Just ask Thelma; she knows!"

March 3, 1994

70. The Essential Qualities of a Pastor

Churches want certain qualities in their pastors, but those qualities don't help predict whether a person will be a good pastor.

Over the years that I have been involved in pastoral ministry concerns, I have collected a wide variety of statements that intend to identify the essential characteristics of a good pastor.

Reading any one of these, most of us would quickly say: "Yes, those are the things we would expect of our pastor." We expect our pastor to know and understand the scriptures, to be a person of prayer, to relate well to people, and so on.

A major research project was done some years ago for the Association of Theological Schools regarding expectations for pastors and their readiness for ministry. The No. 1 qualification identified was the "willingness to serve without the need for acclaim."

That was not to say that pastors don't ever need affirmation for what they do. As a matter of fact, the best way to help your pastor grow is to give a clear word of support for something he or she has done well. Affirmation increases the energy and commitment in all of us, whether we are pastors or not.

But the willingness to serve without the need for acclaim does point to how central is the servanthood stance in good leadership. Jesus understood this better than any of us can hope to achieve, but it is still the goal.

The author of the pastoral epistles also listed qualifications for bishops and deacons, leadership persons in the early church. "Now a bishop must be: (1) above reproach; (2) married only once; (3) temperate; (4) sensible; (5) respectable; (6) hospitable; (7) an apt teacher; (8) not a drunkard; (9) not violent but gentle; (10) not quarrelsome; (11) not a lover of money; (12) must manage his own household well, keeping his children submissive and respectful in every way." (2 Timothy 3:2-4).

That's quite a list. It provides a good beginning to any discussion of qualifications for ministry. If we could talk to the author, I would have some questions for clarification, and I might have a few additional items to suggest. But it is significant to see such an early attempt in the developing Christian church to provide a list of qualifications.

I recently became aware of additional research done by Frank C. Williams in behalf of the Lutheran and Baptist denominations. He made an important distinction that provides a significant understanding of what makes a good minister.

Williams suggested it is important to distinguish between "desirable qualifications" and "predictive qualifications" for ministry. That is to say, churches almost universally want certain qualities in their pastors, but those qualities give almost no help in anticipating whether or not a person will be a good pastor.

Examples of such desirable but non-predictive elements are aspects of personal piety such as humility, biblical grounding, meaningful prayer life, and social conscience. We would not want a pastor in whom these things were missing, but these things in themselves have little to do with predicting whether the pastor will serve effectively.

On the other hand, Williams identified qualities that were predictive. These were useful in determining beforehand whether a pastor would be effective. Such elements included items such as the following: being a self-starter, assertiveness, being a visionary, "stick-to-it-iveness," decisiveness, ability to analyze situations, and flexibility.

"Regardless of polity . . . these were consistently found . . . in those who were effective and were missing in those who were less effective," Williams wrote.

The research done for this project was particularly directed toward qualifications of persons for church planting. But I believe that what makes for an outstanding church planter is not different from what makes for high quality pastoral leadership in traditional congregations. The only difference is that if the essential predictive factors are missing, this becomes evident much more quickly in church planting situations.

Does distinguishing between desirable and predictive elements mean that the church can ignore the desirable side of things since the predictive side is such a powerful indicator of pastoral effectiveness? Of course not. We still want pastors of personal piety and spiritual disciplines. But we ignore the predictive elements only at great risk.

March 17, 1994

71. Wanted: Pastor with What It Takes

It is essential to embrace the pastoral role with a spirit of servanthood as taught and modeled by Jesus.

Is it possible to describe what it takes to be a good and competent pastor? We sometimes act as though it is a great mystery with no answers, except perhaps good luck and the grace of God.

Certainly one part of competent ministry is depending upon God's grace and forbearance with us as human beings. But it is no great mystery to describe what constitutes a competent pastor in our day.

I would begin with the person of the pastor. We expect pastors to have a strong sense of identity; they need to have a sense of being persons of worth, confidence, and self-esteem. They need to understand themselves as persons with whom God has been patient, who have been forgiven by God's grace and made whole.

Pastors must accurately perceive their relationships to others. They cannot carry over into ministry dysfunctional patterns growing out of early injuries to the self.

They must be able to listen to and hear the inner voice of the other person's spirit. If pastors cannot do this with other persons, it is doubtful they can listen to God.

Pastors must accept the unique representational role which they embody for the church. They must embrace and live out the paradox of being one with their people yet separate from them in order to serve them.

It is essential to embrace the pastoral role with a spirit of servanthood as taught and modeled by Jesus. Again a paradox must be accepted and lived out: to lead with authority but not with an authoritarian spirit.

Competent ministers will grow both personally and professionally, thus experiencing ministry as a challenging adventure.

They will embrace many polarities, including both doubt and faith. Thus they will be bridges of understanding, bringing together the incredible diversity within the church and between the church and world.

In their powerful role as leaders, pastors must function with ethical integrity and a clear sense of appropriate boundaries. Today all pastors must accept multiple forms of accountability to other persons and church structures.

A high degree of competence is required of today's pastor. Generally this means a fairly high level of education, somewhere near to equal those to whom the pastor is ministering.

We assume competence in interpreting the Bible, in being theologically and historically literate, and even worldly wise. But competence is more than education. It includes the ability to function effectively in several specific pastoral tasks; these are not optional but essential components of pastoral ministry. I identify three such essential components:

1. Public ministry such as preaching and teaching, which includes the meaningful contemporary interpretation of faith as part of the church's missionary task.

2. Person-to-person ministry in both formal settings such as visitation, or the informal but highly significant contact that occurs throughout the week.

3. Administrative ministry, which includes leadership, vision, organization, and coordination.

Effective pastors will bring energy and discipline to their work. They will be self-starting and have some sense of entrepreneurship. They will not however over-function and control others, nor expect from others what they are themselves unwilling to give. As in every good relationship, there will be an element of sacrifice and flexibility when duty calls.

Even if the pastor is an introvert, she or he will learn to function in an extroverted style when necessary. Even though the pastor is free-flowing and responsive to the moment, he or she will have learned some of the disciplines and rewards of functioning in an organized manner.

Obviously we expect pastors to love and serve Christ without the need for acclaim. They must also love the church, not just the church of their ideals but the living and often all-too-human institution.

Though pastors will carry in their souls the burdens of living in a world and within a church that is not perfect, they will know a joy and contentment that is at peace with themselves, with others, and with God. Of such is the pastoral spirituality which gives birth to faith, hope, and love.

April 7, 1994

72. After a Pastor Retires, What Next?

We think of retirement as the end of something, but it is more healthy to think of it as a transition.

There is no more important task for a minister than to bring the years of Christian ministry to a positive and graceful conclusion. That's what I told a group of about 50 persons, pastors and spouses, who recently gathered in Pennsylvania to discuss the issues of retirement from ministry.

How sad it is to see a person who has given a lifetime to serve Christ and the church come to the close of those years as a bitter and angry person. But it happens far too often.

Perhaps the years of self-giving and sacrificial service finally take their toll. In some cases the pastor has not been able to maintain credibility and competence to the end, but fails to perceive it. Sometimes congregations do cruel and thoughtless things that wound the soul deeply.

Whatever the cause, it is a truly unfortunate day for the pastor and family. It does not serve the health of the congregation, and it represents an apparent failure of the Christian message when a minister in the church does not end things well.

The Pennsylvania group represented those who have committed themselves to planning for a good retirement process. They understood that much of the responsibility is theirs. And they were willing to invest their time and resources to come together and learn from each other.

Society teaches us to think of retirement as the end of something. We think of it as the end of the years of engagement with life through our vocation. In fact, it is far more healthy to think of it in terms of a transition into the third phase of life that offers new opportunities, as well as liabilities.

This third phase of life confronts ministers and all persons with a series of questions. The questions are not new; but the answers need to be.

1. Who am I and what is my role? For ministers their identity, as well as their role, has often become so linked with the church that there is confusion about who they are when ministry is no longer the defining relationship. The ministerial role has brought with it certain forms of power, authority, and responsibility. In retirement these issues are still important, but they must find new answers.

2. Who is my neighbor? Where is home? These questions do not have easy answers for the minister and her or his spouse. Behind the obvious question about where to live is the more serious question about where to find experiences of community and meaningful relationships.

3. Where is meaning to be found? This is the question of what to do with one's time and energy in a way that is personally fulfilling and offers continuing gifts to others and to God's world.

Some, out of necessity or choice, experience retirement as the end of meaningful engagement with life. Others find various options of continuing ministry, including offering to the church the important role of serving in interim/transition pastorates. Still others develop new skills and interests, such as becoming an artist. It can also be a time of serving the church and its institutions as a volunteer.

4. How will I manage my resources? We don't like to admit it, but the truth is that financial resources or the lack of them becomes a fundamental question. It affects every other question and determines the range of options in retirement.

5. Will I abide by the ethics of ministry in retirement? This is one of the most difficult issues for pastors because it is so easy to confuse ministerial relationships and personal friendships. Friendships gained through the years of service to the church can and should continue. But ministerial roles must be relinquished if we care deeply about the church and the next generation of pastors.

Lindon Wenger wrote a book, *Climbing Down the Ladder,* about his own experiences of retirement from ministry. He writes: "The years beyond 65, retirement time, should be the discretionary years—time to choose our activities according to our strength, to continue intellectual adventures, to serve others with a new freedom."

June 2, 1994

73. Politics in the Church

When politics enters the church, we distort the truth about each other. We seek power and control. When we put the church into a win-lose mode, everyone loses.

Pastors must carry within themselves an innate sense of being political. By that I mean we must be alert to and aware of what the majority of members in a congregation will support. Pastors must also be sensitive to things that will cause other persons to take offense.

When pastors do not have a good political sense, things tend to come apart. Unnecessary offense is given to those looking for an excuse to become the disloyal opposition. A divided congregation is the eventual tragic outcome.

Being politically astute is essential to vocational survival, even in the church. That does not mean that pastors should try to calculate every word and action in terms of whether it will win friends and influence people. Putting one's finger to the wind to discern what is currently popular is also phony. There is nothing worse than the leadership person who is perceived as not being authentic and honest.

There are times when pastors must say and do unpopular things. There are occasions when "thus saith the Lord" may not be politically wise, though it is the right and faithful response.

There is a time to be political just as there are times to cast politics aside. The politically-wise pastor knows the difference and obeys the voice of the Spirit.

Does politics belong in the church? The word comes from the Greek suffix for city: *-polis*. Thus it has to do with how we learn to live together in ways that enable complex relationships to stay healthy. The word "polity" is derived from this, and has to do with how we organize ourselves to live peaceably with each other.

Politics has become a negative word in our society. It has connotations of the self-serving and often divisive way in which our government leaders function. Thus politics has to do with short range benefit, often with survival in office. And it has little or nothing to do with wisdom and good leadership.

So does politics belong in the church? Certainly not in the sense of what politics has come to mean today. But there are additional reasons why politics does not belong in church.

As we have come to practice democratic politics, we have cast our lot with a win-lose option. We work aggressively to gain the advantage over others. We seek power and control. We take actions to ensure that our side will win. We campaign to support one side or the other.

So what happens when politics in this sense enters the church? First of all, we lose sight of the common good. We no longer understand the priority of our call from God to our united witness for Christ. Instead of working together for God's mission in the world, we turn inward and struggle with each other.

Politics in the church creates a divided church. And a divided church constitutes a failure of the gospel, which must always work toward reconciliation. (Read once again the books of Ephesians, II Corinthians, and I John.) A divided congregation brings pain and anguish to our common life, to say nothing about the pain which it brings to each member.

When politics enters the church we inevitably distort the truth about each other. We begin to portray ourselves as right and others as wrong. Everyone loses perspective. Everyone believes things about others which are not true. Everyone says and does things that harm and hurt. There is always enough blame to go around.

Instead of seeking to understand each other, politics causes us to seek first to be understood. And that's getting it backwards. When we put the church into a win-lose mode, everyone loses. This is just as true for denominations and church institutions as it is for congregations.

June 30, 1994

74. What Shall We Pay the Pastor?

Congregations perceive conference salary guidelines as maximums. Pastors interpret them as minimums.

It is time once again when pastors and members of the church leadership need to look at the issue of a pastor's salary.

It has become widely understood that salaries need to be adjusted annually. Generally this is done in the fall in preparation for an annual church budget.

Over the years I have made several observations about this process. These observations have become a set of assumptions, almost axioms. They help me to understand why this issue generates such strong feelings, both on the part of pastors and congregations.

1. The economy is always bad at salary setting time! Of course, this is how pastors hear the story from the church. But honestly, that line is so routine that I think that I can safely say, after 30 years of experience, that is what pastors are annually told.

It's not true, of course. In fact these decades have been incredibly prosperous, even when one takes into account inflation and the occasional downturns.

2. Salary guidelines from conferences and denominations are always perceived and interpreted differently. Congregations and those who represent them will invariably perceive these guidelines as maximums.

Pastors, on the other hand, will always interpret these same guidelines as minimums! That fact will cause stress and tension in the relationship and will make communication both difficult and exceedingly necessary.

3. Conferences and denominational offices will understand these salary recommendations as guidelines that call for considerable flexibility in the local setting. They are, after all, nothing more than guidelines, which need appropriate adjustment to geo-

graphical and other environmental conditions. In contrast, both congregations and pastors will tend to read and interpret these guidelines literally and inflexibly, choosing to ignore local situations that might affect either adversely.

4. No one ever takes all the relevant factors into consideration! The reality is that salary determination is a fairly complex issue in our society.

We have made attempts to take into account experience, education, levels of responsibility, and cost of living related to geographical setting. But even then it is difficult to know how to interpret these and other issues that may affect salary determination.

5. Comparisons with other persons and other professions will be made to each party's advantage! I firmly believe that pastors ought to be looked at in terms of the range of what other pastors receive as compensation, rather than to begin by making comparisons with other professions such as those in teaching or educational administration.

But having said that, I know that pastors will and can always find other pastors who are receiving more than they are. Congregations will always be able to make comparisons with other congregations who don't support their pastor "as well as we do."

Salary comparisons are inevitable and occasionally even helpful. But we should always be alert to the distortions, which such comparisons inevitably make.

6. There is no perfect justice; there is only approximate justice when it comes to salary determination. Fairness is never easy to achieve. And even if we did achieve a perfectly just and fair salary for church employees, probably no one would recognize it as such.

While none of us wants to be treated unjustly, we stand a better chance of achieving some approximate level of justice when we seek it for others rather than for ourselves.

7. Since salaries are no longer adjusted according to personal needs, all of us must learn to adjust our needs to the salary we receive.

There was a time when we thought that need should determine salary. If you had 10 children you deserved more salary than the person who had two. If spouses were both employed, they did not need as high a salary.

These assumptions are almost gone in our society, including in the church. They are gone because they also created distortions and unfairness. So all of us, pastors included, must learn to adjust our needs to the salaries we receive.

8. Pastors should and usually do lead by example in Christian financial stewardship. To experience the joy of supporting the church and all the causes one believes in deeply yields spiritual satisfactions beyond words.

Pastors and all others who practice "first fruits giving" know that it is still "more blessed to give than to receive."

August 18, 1994

75. Anonymous Letters Do No Good

Anonymous letters have a profound negative effect on how pastors perceive their relationship to the congregation.

Every pastor has or will receive one sometime. We're talking about unsigned letters. It's not a pleasant subject, but I feel compelled to write about it.

Who writes unsigned letters? Usually it is someone who

feels something intensely and believes that it needs to be shared with the pastor. Almost always the letter is critical of the pastor.

The assumption is that the writer's wisdom will help the pastor to change or to repent. And the assumption is that this will happen by an impersonal confrontation.

The reality is that most often the unsigned letter is nothing more than a way of expressing anger and venting of negative emotions. It often presumes to speak for others in the congregation. But of course they are anonymous, too.

So how does the pastor respond? First of all, it needs to be clear that anonymous letters have a profound negative effect in how pastors perceive their relationship to the congregation. There is always a psychological distancing—not only to the writer who, after all, is unknown—but to the whole relationship.

Pastors know they should not take these letters seriously. In fact, they should be tossed into file 13—the wastebasket. But curiosity and a genuine desire to be open to critique makes that very difficult.

The effect of the anonymous letter is to place a psychological and spiritual scar on the pastor's soul, making effective ministry more difficult. It creates feelings of helplessness and isolation. With whom should the pastor share such information? How can the pastor find assistance in interpreting what is true? Can the pastor trust anyone?

Unsigned letters violate a basic biblical principle of direct, honest, and open confrontation between disagreeing persons in the church. We often refer to it as the principle of Matthew 18. "If another member of the church sins against you, go and point out the fault when the two of you are alone." (Matt. 18:15)

Unable to respond according to Matthew 18, pastors often are tempted to respond in other ways. Since the writer has not had the courage to identify himself or herself privately, the pastor may respond by deciding that the letter is public information.

Pastors have been known to tear up the unsigned letter in front of the congregation, thus symbolizing that they will not be intimidated by this un-Christian communication.

This week I heard of two other responses. One self-assured pastor posted the unsigned letter on the church's bulletin board, challenging the author to sign it if it was to be taken seriously and responded to appropriately. Another read the letter publicly!

I don't suggest these are the best ways to handle unsigned communications. That is to respond by ridicule and intimidation, which is hardly more appropriate that writing such letters in the first place. But having received such letters myself, I understand the temptations to respond in this way.

In the church we are all called to be truthful and open with each other. "But speaking the truth in love, we must grow up in every way into him who is the head, into Christ." (Eph. 4:15)

September 1, 1998

76. Don't Forget the Unwritten Rules

Tacit agreements either give energy and life to a relationship or become the basis for failure and unmet expectations.

My friend and colleague Erick Sawatzky recently shared a concept with a group that I found very insightful—and possibly even important—in explaining what often goes wrong for us in relationships. Erick was speaking about covenants and contracts which form our agreements about how we will relate with each other.

The distinction which Erick made was the difference between explicit agreements and tacit agreements. Let me explain. Explicit agreements are those covenants or contracts which are so clear to both parties that they are spoken and very often written down. Everybody knows and understands what the agreement entails and what can be expected from each other in the relationship.

Explicit agreements can be changed through negotiation. Thus a contract can be adjusted to the new circumstances which affect the relationship. These explicit covenants help us to know what to expect and how to live up to these expectations. They are the oil that helps our relationships run smoothly and effectively.

Tacit agreements, on the other hand, are neither spoken or written. They operate silently, but they are nevertheless very powerful. My dictionary defines tacit as something "not expressed or declared openly, but implied." Tacit agreements are those expectations we have of each other, even though we never talk about them.

How might these two forms of covenants, explicit and tacit, be understood in the relationship between the pastor and the congregation?

In recent history we have learned how important and helpful it is to develop several explicit agreements between a pastor and congregation. We try to do this right at the beginning of the commitment to avoid misunderstandings and to establish a long-term agreement that will be positive and healthy.

Two explicit contracts which are expected today are: (1) a job description; and (2) a memo of understanding. In effect the job description is the agreement of what the pastor promises to provide for the congregation. It details some of these expectations such as preaching, providing pastoral care, and certain tasks of administration.

On the other hand the Memo of Understanding is a contract of what the congregation promises to provide for the pastor in terms of a salary, vacation, health insurance, retirement benefits, etc.

Both of these explicit agreements can and should be

changed from time to time. The wise congregation will review the Memo of Understanding annually and bring it up to date; it might be wise to review the job description in the same way to make sure that these explicit agreements are still in effect and being met.

But what about the tacit agreements between pastors and congregations? How do we learn what they are? These are the expectations and promises which often get us into trouble. Remember that they are not spoken or written but still very much expected.

Let me try to describe some typical tacit covenants which form the relationship between a pastor and a congregation. Pastors promise and the congregations expect that pastors will deal honestly and carefully with every relationship.

Pastors promise and people expect that pastors can be trusted not to harm or injure the body, soul, or spirit of another. Pastors promise and members expect that the pastor will maintain confidential information. But all these promises and expectations are unwritten and usually unspoken.

On the other hand, congregations promise and pastors expect that the congregation will be supportive and responsive to the gospel. Congregations covenant that they will be reasonable in their expectations of the pastor's time and work.

Congregations agree to find the delicate balance between respecting the office of ministry which they give to their pastor while not putting the pastor on a pedestal of impossible expectations. Congregations expect that pastors will be sensitive to and appreciative of their unique traditions, even while challenging them to new visions and possibilities.

These and a multitude of other tacit agreements either give energy and life to this relationship or they can become the basis for failure and unmet expectations. Can you describe other tacit agreements that are operative in your congregation?

December 1, 1994

77. "Amen" to These Pastoral Prayers

Most pastors don't think of themselves as artists. I think they should. Their medium is words.

One of the weekly challenges every pastor faces is the weekly pastoral prayer. If this is not an issue, it probably means that the pastor has accepted a repetition of words and phrases that are almost routine.

Others seek to respond to the challenge of creatively crafting words that capture the imagination, calling the congregation to be engaged in the prayer with the pastor. When that happens authentically, the pastoral prayer becomes the prayer of the congregation.

That should be the goal of the pastoral prayer. At the first level it is the prayer spoken by the pastor. But in its more profound meaning it is the prayer which the congregation prays with the pastor.

To lead in prayer in that manner takes preparation. It means being sufficiently in touch with the congregation that one's spirit is prepared to put into words what they think and feel but often cannot express. It is a spirituality disciplined in the everyday life of the world.

Prayers that have enabled me to pray with the pastor have often had the power of poetry. Their use of language has also been disciplined by preparation and careful, imaginative thought. There is rhythm and flow. There is movement and progression. There is a beginning, a climax, and an ending.

The best example of prayers as poetry are the Psalms. The authors of these prayers have used all sorts of literary techniques to engage our senses creatively. The most basic characteristic of Hebrew poetry is what scholars have called parallelism—the repetition of the same basic idea with differing words in successive lines.

So we have a biblical example of prayer as poetry that can

serve as a model for what we ought to expect of pastors. Yes, it takes discipline and hard work and preparation. But the pastoral prayer is an offering to God and to the congregation—the gift of a pastor's imagination and creativity.

Most pastors don't think of themselves as artists. I think they should. The tools of a pastor's art are not paint and brush and canvas. They are paper and pen and computer, and the medium is words.

Pastoral prayers can take several directions. All of us have at times heard a prayer that was a disguised sermon. The pastor has tried to use the prayer to make a point not with God but with the people who hear it.

That is to miss the point. The psalmist used prayers to make a point, usually to offer a complaint. But they were always directed to God. Using the pastoral prayer as a disguised sermon is a misuse, trying to use God to bless and impose our values.

A second common type of pastoral prayer is one that reaffirms the accepted traditions and beliefs, reenforcing truth that is known.

There is certainty and confidence in hearing again and again that things have not changed with God. Most of us have enough doubts that make such re-enforcement and reaffirmation needed and helpful, even if the prayer does little to stir us beyond our present understandings.

A third type of pastoral prayer captures my "amen" response. These are the pastoral prayers that stretch and challenge me to still greater thought and understanding. They take me to the borders of my imagination and ask me to look just beyond that. I am invited to take the risk of discovery beyond the ordinary and expected and already understood.

Our pastor invited us into such a journey recently in a pastoral prayer. He took us into the vast reaches of the universe which the Hubbell telescope is now discovering, addressing God and asking whether there might be those in other galaxies in need of the Savior and whether Christ had come there as the incarnate Son of God!

The poetry of that prayer had power to stretch my theological imagination. The pastoral prayer became my prayer, the prayer of the congregation.

On a recent Sunday at the close of the pastoral prayer I heard behind me a very quiet but still audible "amen." That came both as a surprise and an affirmation that the pastoral prayer had become again the prayer of the people, eliciting a heartfelt response.

One doesn't have to say "amen" audibly, but I hope you do at least occasionally say "amen" to yourself and to God at the conclusion of the pastor's—the congregation's—prayer.

January 19, 1995

78. Constitutions Get Us Organized

Most congregations need three leadership groups: a church board or council, deacons or elders, and commissions or committees.

Why do congregations write constitutions and sometimes by-laws? I suspect it has something to do with: the shortness and failure of human memory (we forget how we did it the last time); the need to control power (so that certain strong persons don't dominate); and to deal with growing complexity (responsibilities must be defined and shared).

Structures and systems are important to every human organization, including the church. We need constitutions to enable us to live together in ways that simplify our relationships, that create a dependable routine, and that help to ensure responsible leadership and trusting "followership."

I receive quite a few requests for advice about writing constitutions. I'm not really an expert on this topic; but no one else in our system is, either. So I sometimes send out a sample of one congregational constitution which I rather like and which has proved workable over an extended period of time.

What have I learned about church constitutions over several decades of church involvement?

1. Keep it simple and workable. You will never define or describe every conceivable new issue which the congregation may need to resolve, so don't even try. Provide a basic structure that allows for flexible response.

2. Make it fit your congregation. The smaller the congregation the less structure is needed or wanted. A new church looking toward growth can define the structure in such a way that people and positions are added as the membership grows.

It is infinitely more difficult to simplify a structure in a congregation declining in membership, but it should be done.

3. I like to see a division between the constitution and a set of bylaws. The constitution can serve as an identity document, defining who you are and the nature of your relationships. The constitution can be quite brief and intended for longer duration.

The bylaws are more functional, describing how you operate. They are more easily changed. Bylaws may contain membership understandings and procedures. They define boards, commissions, and committees, and how they are chosen. They usually say something about the choosing of pastoral leadership.

Bylaws should also say something about congregational meetings and the decision-making procedures which are anticipated.

4. My sense is that we are moving away from the old form of voting between two or more candidates for office. This is being replaced by gift discernment or appointment systems. In the congregation I attend, most leadership positions are now appointed by a

personnel selection committee. It appears to be working quite well, and it offers the opportunity to move away from popularity contests toward broader involvement of many members.

5. Most congregations, except the very smallest, need three leadership groups. First, a church board or council can be an overall administrative and decision-making body. It can also serve in a coordinating role, helping to hold the whole together.

Second, a group often referred to as deacons or elders can provide spiritually sensitive direction to the congregation and wise counsel to the pastor.

Third, commissions or committees give leadership to specific program areas of the church's life.

6. Constitutions are made to serve the church; not the church for constitutions! We have all known situations where legalistically-minded members use constitutions to defend their traditionalism or use them in hopes of resolving conflict. This usually increases the level of conflict.

Constitutions need to be taken seriously; but time changes all things. And if the constitution becomes an enslavement, then perhaps it is time to draft a new one.

August 3, 1995

79. Is Pastoral Ministry Possible?

Is pastoral ministry an impossible responsibility today? No. Hundreds of examples in our congregations prove to me that persons can and do thrive in ministry.

We were driving from the local airport on a visit I made to a congregation earlier in the year. The driver was a long-time, committed, and active member of his congregation. I know him as an honest, clear thinking, and highly intuitive leader in that church.

His words to me were strong, sharp like a two-edged sword, and spoken out of careful observation and experience: "There is no church so bad that it will not benefit from a competent and spiritually healthy pastor." He paused for a moment and then went on.

"And there is no church so strong that it can withstand the destructive effects of a dysfunctional and incompetent pastor."

There was no need to tell any stories. No diagrams or pictures were added. Painful as it was, I knew that his words were perceptive and true. Leadership is not the only issue in our time. We have a crisis today with "followership."

In our contemporary cynicism, drawn deeply from the wells of our culture, we have made leadership a very difficult task. Levels of trust are low. Where there is no followership, leadership is impossible whether in politics, business, or the church.

But having acknowledged that, it is still true that the single most significant factor in developing healthy, thriving congregations is a well-functioning, competent, spiritually alive pastor, who brings intelligence, personal sensitivity, and energy to the tasks of ministry.

Such a pastor can claim authority without becoming an authoritarian. Such a pastor will live an incarnational presence with people who will know the pastor to be authentically human, even as the pastor lays claim to the church's office of ministry and the representational role all leadership embodies.

I don't like theology formed by slogans. They are usually half-truths, intended to elicit emotional rather than thoughtful responses. But some time ago a slogan on somebody's T-shirt caught my eye. It read: "Get it right or get left." That defines the reality of our age, in terms of vocational competence.

Is pastoral ministry an impossible responsibility today? No. Hundreds of examples in our congregations prove to me that persons can and do thrive in ministry.

Recently I have rejoiced with a series of reports of strong affirmative pastoral votes calling and recalling pastors to continuing ministry in our congregations. I know it can be done. And when it is done well, the church responds accordingly.

Serving in pastoral ministry can be a highly rewarding experience. I like to think of it as a gift given to us by God and the church.

If you seek to be involved with people in some of the most significant moments of their lives, literally from birth to death, pastoral ministry may be for you. If you love people of all ages as much as you love those your own age, pastoral ministry may be for you.

If you seek variety and creativity in your vocation, pastoral ministry may be for you. If you look for a calling that struggles with ultimate questions about the meaning of life, about the course of history, and about eternal truth, pastoral ministry may be for you.

If you need challenges to lifelong learning and growth, pastoral ministry may be for you. If you thrive on moving back and forth between significant relationships and challenging ideas and study, pastoral ministry may be for you.

If you love to read and write and speak, pastoral ministry may be for you. If you love people and are willing to stay in touch with their lives, if you love God and long to be in communion with the Eternal One, pastoral ministry may be for you.

July 20, 1995

80. Character: The Essential Quality

Whereas competence shows what we can do, character reveals who we are. It is that old being and doing issue again.

Our age is showing. My wife Bernice and I recently made trips to participate in 40th class reunions. My journey was to Reedley, Calif., where in 1955 I graduated from Immanuel High School.

Among the numerous renewed acquaintances, one encounter stands out for its significance to my life and work today. Marlow Enns was a good friend back in high school, but we had not seen each other for all these 40 years.

Marlow's work in education as a school principal and my work in pastoral ministry led us quickly to common interests—issues having to do with personnel.

In that conversation, Marlow made a statement that has been etched into my memory: "When I look at hiring teachers I look for two things: character and competence. In that order. Because if you have competence but not character, it will come back to bite you every time."

Instantly I recognized that 40 years had led us to common understandings about the basic issues that matter in education and in church.

Unfortunately, our time together was so brief that we were unable to pursue in greater detail what we both meant by character and competence. But I continue to ask myself and others to clarify what these words mean.

Competence is not difficult to define. We recognize it when it's there, and we know incompetence when we see it. Competence has to do with doing things well and doing things right. It is based on accumulated knowledge and experience, which enables people to act in ways that leave us fulfilled and satisfied. "Excellence" is the word we often use today to describe it.

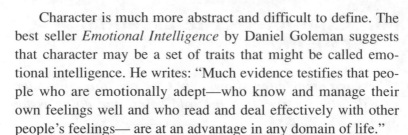

Character is much more abstract and difficult to define. The best seller *Emotional Intelligence* by Daniel Goleman suggests that character may be a set of traits that might be called emotional intelligence. He writes: "Much evidence testifies that people who are emotionally adept—who know and manage their own feelings well and who read and deal effectively with other people's feelings— are at an advantage in any domain of life."

Whereas competence shows what we can do, character reveals who we are. It's that old being-and-doing issue again. The being factor is at the heart of spirituality.

When I think about character, I think of ethics. I think about honesty and commitment to fairness and justice. Other words we use to define character are "integrity" and "authenticity." Both of these are related to honesty. But they are the internal marks of honesty with oneself rather than with others. They point in the direction of an internal consistency and wholeness to life.

Authenticity has to do with being the person we truly are, without phoniness or pretense. In its most negative form, the lack of this kind of character was described in biblical language as hypocrisy.

Another internal quality that has a high priority in my understanding is perception. This is the capacity to see life, oneself, and others both clearly and accurately.

But the importance of perception goes further in our capacity to see issues, to see opportunities, to sense responsibilities, and ultimately to see the universe and God for what and who they are. Does that make character a spiritual issue, or what?

The other word today for perception is "vision." But here we must be careful to define vision as the capacity to see things for what they are and what they might become—not the popular but often misguided notion of vision as imaginary and hoped-for dreams about the future.

The qualities of character that put one in touch with oneself include the capacity for both self-worth and humility. As these qualities are directed toward others, altruism and trust will show themselves.

Finally, character will manifest itself in the capacity to make appropriate decisions about oneself, relationships, and responsibilities.

A biblical word that sums up much of this is from James 3:17: "But the wisdom from above is first pure, then peaceable, gentle, willing to yield, full of mercy and good fruits, without a trace of partiality or hypocrisy." Now that's character.

November 16, 1995

81. Christmas Carols Fit Advent, Too

It seems the whole world is thinking about Christmas, and you hear Christmas music everywhere—except in church.

Why don't we sing Christmas carols in church during Advent?

If you're part of a congregation that observes Advent with a ritual such as lighting the candles of the Advent wreath, and if your pastor preaches on Advent themes for those Sundays, the chances are pretty good that you'll be singing the songs of Advent rather than Christmas carols right up until Christmas eve.

There's nothing wrong with that, of course. Except it seems as though the whole world is thinking about Christmas and you hear Christmas music everywhere—except in church.

Pastors generally love Advent. I always found it much easier to preach on Advent themes than on Christmas. Advent is filled with uncertainty, pathos, and mystery. It has contrasts of light and darkness, hopes fulfilled and hopes dashed to pieces, doubt and faith, the ancient faith of Israel and the dawn of Christian faith.

Advent is about longings. We all have them, don't we? Much of life is about anticipation. Dreams almost always are better than the reality anyhow.

Advent plays to our hopes and dreams, now relived through the stories of the ancient prophets whose words were about their longings for a nation and a people who perpetually seemed to lose their way. And where was God in this uncertain history? These are rich sources for preachers.

Advent songs are sometimes in minor keys to reflect these longings: "O come, O come Emmanuel, and ransom captive Israel, that mourns in lonely exile here, until the Son of God appear."

Well, if you're going to observe the four Sundays of Advent before Christmas day, how better to do it than to sing the songs of hope and longing? Christmas carols don't fit. Ask any pastor. I know. I've been there; done that. But I was never quite comfortable with this pattern.

Now that I've made one confession, let me make another. By the time Christmas arrives in our modern culture, surrounded with the music of the media, I confess to having had enough already, thank you. I'm quite ready to hear and sing other music.

But that leaves most of us shortchanged. At least in church. Advent songs are sung through Advent. Christmas carols are sung on Christmas eve and Christmas day, and maybe the Sunday after. But that's about it.

So what have I done? I've never been an Advent purist. It's always been my hunch that I was not alone in wanting to sing at least one Christmas carol on the Sundays preceding Christmas.

Perhaps it has to do with familiarity and simplicity. You don't even have to grow up in church to learn Christmas carols. Sitting in the pew, as I do most Sundays these days, I can safely acknowledge the joy that comes with singing the familiar.

It's not that I never want to be challenged by the new songs of faith. But there is security—or shall we call it faith?— that is nourished by that which I know and can readily affirm.

I'm not going to lead a crusade to reform the order of Advent and Christmas worship. But just in case you were wondering why you sing so few Christmas carols in church during Advent, I thought you might like to know.

And for now—a blessed and joyful Christmas to all. "O come, let us adore Him, Christ the Lord."

December 21, 1995

82. Can't Afford a Full-Time Pastor?

Congregations often assume they have only two options: support a full-time pastor or close their doors.

I recently participated in a meeting of denominational leaders in Kansas, where we were considering the issue of finding pastoral leadership in small, mostly rural congregations. It is an issue for all denominations in North America.

Congregations often assume they have only two options: support a full-time pastor or close their doors. In reality there are many more options. They require creative thinking, an openness to new ideas, and a willingness to take realistic responsibility to act.

As an outcome of the meeting, I developed a list of 16 options that the smaller congregations might pursue when thinking creatively about pastoral leadership:

1. Seek realistic opportunities to grow, increasing the membership and thus the financial resources to continue to support a full-time pastor.

2. Work hard on stewardship in the hope of raising the level of financial giving so that funds becomes available to continue full-time ministerial leadership.

3. Search for a pastor willing to work in ministry part time, perhaps one who has a spouse who would be employed full time.

4. Search for a pastor willing to live off of Social Security plus the allowable income between the ages of 62 and 70.

5. Search for a pastor who might serve two or more congregations of your denomination in your geographical area.

6. Search for a bivocational pastor with regular pastoral training and experience who is willing to seek other part-time work to supplement his or her income.

7. Search for a bivocational pastor who is trained in two professions and is willing to pursue both as part time positions with two different employers.

8. Search for a bivocational pastor who has primary training and employment in another vocation but is capable of and willing to serve part time in ministry.

9. Call a lay person in your congregation to serve in a part time ministry role, recognizing his or her character and competence for leadership.

10. Form a lay ministry team in the congregation that might share the overall responsibilities with differing people assuming different roles and tasks.

11. Merge your congregation with another congregation near you of your own denomination.

12. Develop a relationship with a larger congregation near you that might provide part-time ministerial leadership to your congregation, as well.

13. Hire a beginning pastor at the entry-level salary so as to lower costs.

14. Develop an ecumenical shared ministry across denominational lines, with one pastor serving two or more congregations of differing denominations in your community.

15. Form a single federated congregation out of two congregations of differing denominations with dual denominational membership.

16. Hope for a conference subsidy to bail you out—an increasingly unlikely possibility.

There are always more options when we allow ourselves to think creatively. You may not like these options, but what are your alternatives? What might be the benefits and the liabilities to any of the above?

January 18, 1996

83. Why I Believe in the Church

In the church I have found, as nowhere else, a genuine and honest quest to make sense of life in all its dimensions.

I believe in the church. Those words may sound strange.

It would seem to make more sense to say: "I believe in what the church teaches," or simply: "I belong to the church." But to say "I believe in the church" seems to say too much.

However, that is what we confess in the Apostles Creed, where we say: "I believe in the holy catholic (meaning the holy

183

universal) church." In this ancient confession we say that we believe in the church the same way that we believe in God.

Here are five reasons why I believe in the church:

1. The church is a place of grace and salvation.

God's grace does not come to us by magic nor by our wishful imagination. It does not come out of thin air or out of nowhere. In divine wisdom God has entrusted to the church the responsibility to be both the preserver and the mediator of the gospel.

Why did God choose such a human institution? I do not know. But I do know that without the church to bear the glorious message of grace and salvation, we would have remained without God and without hope.

I believe in the church because, through it, we have received the divine message of eternal life.

2. The church is a place of community and relationship.

Acknowledging that we sometimes experience pain and alienation even in the church, I still claim that the church, as nowhere else in our world, holds the promise to establish community. Loving acceptance, forgiveness, reconciliation—these words describe the church at its best.

I believe in the church because, through it, we experience friendships and relationships that bridge the barriers that often divide us and isolate us from one another.

3. The church is the place of discovery and growth.

Again, I know that sometimes there is a shadow side, which in the name of truth causes minds to close and hearts to harden.

But I also know myself and my own temptation to see life and faith too narrowly. In the church I am forced to look at things not only from my point of view. With the help and challenge of others I can, if only dimly, begin to catch the breadth and length and height and depth of God's wisdom.

I believe in the church because there resides in it a perspective that pushes me to see beyond this material world, with its limited perspectives on reality. It offers us the opportunity to use both our minds and our spirits in the pursuit of truth.

4. The church is a place of service and opportunity. Most of us don't begin there, at least not today. People seem to be looking to the church for what they can get out of it. If it doesn't meet their full expectations and more, they get out!

But deep inside, most of us know that we receive more in giving than in receiving. Life is made more abundant not by what we have but by what we have the opportunity to share.

The church has an almost infinite capacity to call us to be giving people, to serve through our abilities and with our time, to offer our treasures of wealth and wisdom to others.

I believe in the church because, like prayer, it gives me the opportunity to expand my universe to a world beyond my backyard, beyond my family, and beyond my community.

5. The church is a place of meaning and hope.

Not always, mind you. But in the big picture, which is the perspective most characteristic of God, the church seeks to be the place where we grapple with the big questions.

When the church does its work well, we seek to find meaning in suffering and even in death. Sometimes our answers are trivial, too easy and thoughtless. But then again, in the church I have found, as nowhere else, a genuine and honest quest to make sense of life in all its dimensions.

I believe in the church because it has given me meaning and hope in a world so often without purpose and even more often frivolous in its quest for meaning in life.

February 15, 1996

84. Administration of Money Is Not Optional

The quality of our leadership is most adequately tested in how we do the ministry of administration.

Let's talk about money today. I believe that one part of a pastor's job is to help the congregation to become financially responsible, wise, accountable, and spiritually healthy. That's a tall order.

Are pastors achieving this? I recently reviewed a report entitled *The Reluctant Steward*, which grew out of a stewardship and development study co-sponsored by Christian Theological Seminary and Saint Meinrad Seminary. The results of their study, while not very encouraging, are very instructive.

Ninety-one percent of Protestant pastors surveyed reported being very or extremely satisfied with their role as a pastor. Eighty-one percent felt the same positive response to their pastoral duties and 84 percent with their theological duties.

But when they were asked about their administrative duties and financial duties the positive responses fell to 25 percent and 34 percent.

Reporting on the level of satisfaction with their seminary training in regard to theological and liturgical issues, Protestant pastors were 78 percent very satisfied. These percentages, however, dropped precipitously regarding the level of satisfaction with seminary training in other areas: pastoral duties—52 percent; administrative duties—13 percent; financial duties—seven percent!

When asked about the importance of the seminary offering courses on stewardship, leadership, and management, 68 percent said that this would be very or extremely important. When you add the response of "somewhat important" the percentage rose to 95 percent.

But, when asked about their own interest in taking these courses, the percentages of those very or extremely interested dropped for specific areas as follows: change in the modern congregation— 40 percent; theology of Christian stewardship—26 percent; financial resource management—15 percent .

The principal conclusion of those who conducted the above research was this: "Catholic and Protestant clergy are frustrated by (and feel ill-prepared for) the administrative tasks that are an increasingly demanding part of their pastoral responsibilities.

"However, in spite of this frustration—and their conviction that seminaries should do a better job of preparing future ministers for leadership, management, and stewardship of the church's resources—pastors do not express an interest in learning more about the administrative and financial aspect of their ministries through continuing education courses, seminars, or other training programs."

Having read hundreds of Mennonite pastor's files in which they suggest their pastoral priorities, I know this research reflects our experience, as well. As further evidence, two recent Pastor's Week experiences in Canada and United States brought significantly less enrollment when the theme for the week dealt with stewardship.

I have come to several convictions about things relating to pastors, administration, and church finance.

1. Administration is not busy work. It is ministry. We ought to talk about the pastoral ministry of administration.

2. Administration is not optional. A pastor cannot decide not to do it or to have someone else do it. It may not be your strong suit, but you must pay attention to it.

3. The quality of our leadership is most adequately tested not in our public ministry but in how we do the ministry of administration. Whether we have a vision that guides our work will become most evident in how we do the administrative side of ministry, not in how well we preach.

4. It is wrong to define stewardship so narrowly that it deals with only money. It is equally wrong to define stewardship so broadly that we ignore financial issues.

5. Pastors can help congregations become more financially

responsible. Pastors have the duty to make a positive difference. But to prove themselves credible, they must be willing to learn.

March 7, 1996

85. Whole Greater Than the Sum of Parts

A pastor is one of the last generalists. A visionary leaders must be someone who sees the whole.

While talking with seminary students recently, I found myself saying several times: "Pastoral ministry is a vocation where the whole is greater than the sum of its parts."

So what prompted that response? Several things which I have been hearing in recent years from prospective pastors such as: "I really enjoy planning and leading worship," or "I would like to work at spiritual direction with the congregation," or "I would like to preach more, but don't ask me to be a youth pastor," or "I am focusing on pastoral counseling in my study, but I'm not a preacher," or "I have a gift for organization and administration; somebody else will need to do pastoral visitation."

What each of these views communicates is that ministry can be sliced up in an infinite variety of ways. Since many tasks need to be done, we can divide these up among several people so that each one can do what they do best or like best.

The rationale for this approach to ministry goes something like this: No pastor has all the gifts for ministry. In fact the "gifts passages" of Romans, Ephesians, and 1 Corinthians contain the expectation that the spiritual gifts will be spread around. Since no pastor has all the gifts, the church can discern who is called to do what.

In interpreting these texts we often forget the context. The issue Paul is addressing grows out of diversity and conflict in the church. The image of the variety of gifts is his way of responding to diversity.

He is saying that with all our differences we can see that everyone is contributing to the common good. Diversity is not bad. It is God's way of helping us to envision a larger unity.

No pastor can do everything, nor do everything equally well. Ministry at its best is always shared. All God's people are called to ministry.

But I want to hold out for a view of pastoral ministry that sees the whole as always being more than the sum of its parts. Serving as a pastor cannot be cut up into a series of things to be done.

Why? Because pastoring has more to do with being than with doing.

A pastor is one of the last generalists. In an age of specialization where jobs are divided into narrow fields of interest, the pastor is called to a vocation that is multifaceted, and that calls for a variety of complementary gifts. A visionary leader must be someone who sees the whole.

Another way of talking about this is to ask: Who cares for the soul of the congregation? Who sees that congregation as a whole? Who brings into a common focus the present, the past, and the future? Who seeks to nurture and care for the congregational system and the congregational self?

Certainly not someone whose responsibility it is to do one or two tasks that are needed at the moment.

To be a pastor is to claim this whole. It is to offer oneself as a whole person for a whole ministry, in which the whole is greater than the sum of its parts.

November 7, 1996

86. Isn't a Verbal Agreement Enough?

Not putting these things in writing invites misunderstanding, hard feelings, and, in some situations, conflict.

"Why should we treat our pastor as if he is like an employee? I thought that a pastor was supposed to be in a covenant relationship with the congregation. That means we ought to be able to trust one another, doesn't it? Why do we need to put this all down in writing?"

I continue to be surprised by the number of times I come across situations where there is no written agreement between the pastor and the congregation. Usually this is in situations where things have always been done by verbal agreements. After all, wasn't a person's word as good as one's bond?

A written agreement between a pastor and a congregation is necessary to formalize the relationship. It suggests that certain things are expected of each other. In the case of a Covenant of Understanding, this is an agreement about what the pastor can expect from the church.

Included in this "contract" are items such as salary for the current year, vacation time allowance, health care coverage, retirement fund deposits, provision for conference participation, reimbursement policies such as mileage for church-related travel, and sabbatical agreements. These are items which the church agrees to provide for the pastor.

But there is another side—what the pastor agrees to provide for the church. We call this a job description. Included in such a list are congregational expectations regarding pastoral responsibilities such as preaching and worship leadership, providing pastoral care for the congregation through visitation and counseling, and administrative duties.

We expect today that these be written documents, formal agreements negotiated and signed by the proper persons.

We have learned by hard experience that it is not sufficient to trust the memory of persons regarding these important agreements. Those who made the original commitment may die or leave the position. Memory is often faulty and simply cannot be trusted over the course of a year or longer.

Not putting these things into writing invites misunderstanding, hard feelings, and, in some situations, conflict.

We put these things into writing precisely because we want to trust and care for each other. We want to make clear our good will and intention regarding this relationship between a pastor and a congregation.

Yes, the pastor is an employee of the church and deserves to be treated responsibly and fairly. I often hear that the pastor should not be treated as an employee. I don't agree.

I do agree that a pastor is more than just an employee. The relationship with the congregation is also that of a covenant. This is a spiritual relationship that must be more than a contractual agreement for services.

This relationship is that of an employee with additional levels of meaning above that. But that additional level of understanding does not negate the employee-employer relationship . We must lay the foundation upon which the larger relationship can grow and prosper.

February 20, 1997

87. A Perfectionist Pastor's Blunder

There is considerable grace, forgiveness, and even good humor in the unintentional error.

"Look at what is before your eyes." *(2 Corinthians 10:7)*

It was the end of a fairly ordinary week. As a pastor I had learned years before that it paid to work ahead. So my basic schedule called for completing sermon preparation on Thursday.

That discipline had a number of advantages. If, for some reason, the sermon preparation ran into trouble, I still had Friday as a back-up. But if I completed the sermon on Thursday, Friday was really a good day.

I could begin with the morning at the office, catching up on things that tended to be put off. The afternoon called for visitation, normally with a stop at the local hospital. On my way home it was my responsibility to pick up the bulletins from the local print shop owned by a member of the congregation.

Being thoughtful and helpful (at least I thought I was), it was my custom to stop by the organ with my load of bulletins so that I could leave a bulletin for the organist who would come to rehearse on Saturday morning. After walking through the sanctuary, the next stop was to place my load of bulletins by the main entry, ready for distribution on Sunday.

This had been a good Friday. I was even a bit ahead of schedule, with the anticipation of Friday evening at home. It was my rule not to schedule church events on Friday evening. That was an important family night both for our family and others in the church.

As I walked into the side entrance of the church, the organ was being played. But that was nothing unusual. Bethel College organ students routinely practiced on our church organ, and we welcomed that cooperative relationship.

Entering the chancel from the side, in my happy anticipation of what lay ahead, I marched around the organ, pulled out a bulletin, and, with an extra gesture, placed it upon the organ. I did notice a strange smile from the student organist, who just kept on playing.

Not gaining any further attention from her, I turned to make my way to the back of the sanctuary with several boxes of bulletins in hand. Coming to the chancel steps I looked up—and behold: an entire sanctuary full of people, with all the college music faculty in the front rows attentively listening to a student recital and watching my ill-timed antics.

"Look at what is before your eyes!"

What to do? My first impulse was to continue my way down the center aisle. No, I couldn't do that. So I did a quick turn to my right and, like a football halfback, slithered my way to the sidelines and out the door. And out of the church, thoroughly embarrassed. That evening was recovery time for the wounded ego of a pastor who tended toward perfectionism and didn't do things like that.

I learned two things that Friday. 1) Don't make assumptions based upon past experiences. Pay attention to present reality. Or in the out-of-context words of Paul: "Look at what is before your eyes." 2) There is considerable grace, forgiveness, and even good humor in the unintentioned error.

Prayer: Lord, grant to us as large a measure of grace in our relationships with others as we need grace in our relationship to you. Help us to pay attention to what's happening all around us every day. Amen.

May 15, 1997

88. You Can't Clone Your Old Pastor

Pastors are as different as everyone in the congregation. Fortunate is the congregation that welcomes that difference.

Ever since scientists announced they had cloned a sheep, there has been rising interest and concern that this new development would be applied to human beings.

I experience the interest in cloning quite often among our congregations. It goes something like this:

A well loved pastor has served a congregation many years and led it toward growth, both spiritually and numerically. This pastor eventually leaves, perhaps retiring or to assume a new responsibility in the work of God's kingdom. The congregation grieves the loss; and it is right and good that they do so.

But now they must plan for the future. The search process begins with the hope and expectation that God will provide new leadership. It should happen as soon as possible, since the congregation does not want to lose momentum.

The congregation names a search committee. They work with their conference minister. They complete the expected congregational information forms. And they attempt to identify the type of pastor they believe is needed to follow the well beloved pastor. Who and what are they looking for? A clone!

I have news for congregations looking for clones. God doesn't make them! Twins, occasionally. But if they are both pastors, they usually have the wisdom not to follow each other in the same congregation.

It's good God doesn't make clones. Pastors are unique and special. They are as different as everyone in the congregation. They come to us with different ideas, different ways of doing the same job, different emphases, different styles.

Fortunate is the congregation that anticipates and welcomes that difference. They will continue to grow, though not always in ways they anticipate.

One of the best ways to assist a congregation with this pastoral transition is to have an interim or transition pastor. This is a pastor who is committed to help a congregation move beyond the "clone syndrome."

Often congregations assume that they don't need an interim pastor if they have ended the relationship with the well beloved pastor without conflict. Isn't it only highly conflicted congregations which need interim ministry to resolve difficult issues?

The answer is no. Congregations making healthy transitions to new pastoral leadership can avoid the clone effect by choosing to experience the ministry of someone who will help them make the transition. A year is normally needed to benefit from the positive effects of interim or transition ministry.

Ralph Colby, director of the Interim Pastors Network, recently described the interim pastor as a "faster pastor." It takes a highly skilled person to engage quickly with a congregation in this important transition process.

The biblical model for the interim or transition pastor is John the Baptist. He was a servant of God who prepared the way for the one who was to follow. And there were no clones in that transition.

June 19,1997

195

89. Advice for Pastors on the Move

The time to seek a new call is when things are going well in your present ministry—not when they have begun to fall apart.

Fifty thousand pastors make a geographical and congregational move each year. That statistic is on the first page of a book dealing with pastoral transition: *Opening the Clergy Parachute: Soft Landings for Church Leaders Who Are Seeking a Change* by Christopher C. Moore.

The purpose of the book is to offer counsel and assistance to pastors who are contemplating or making a move from one church to another. This is a "how-to" book for pastors rather than for congregational search committees. If you need help in this process, read this book.

Moore makes numerous points that I agree with. Some go contrary to the presumed wisdom of others. Here are several examples:

- "A natural transition point occurs at some time between the seventh and 11th years in a current ministry."
- "The golden years for placement in a new ministry are 35 to 45. Opportunities begin to restrict after 50 and, at 55, even a lateral move may be difficult."
- "If at all possible, do not— repeat, do not—resign your present position until you have accepted a new call, no matter how strong the pressure to resign may be."
- "As a general rule, the time to seek a new call is when things are going well in your present ministry—not when they have begun to fall apart."
- "It is important to realize that you will always have to deal with difficult people in ministry (or in any employment that engages people)."
- "The general appearance of your profile is extremely impor-

tant. Make sure the information you present is neat, legible, and concise."

- "Your effectiveness as a candidate depends in no small part upon your continued effectiveness where you are."
- "Research has shown that people gain their first impression of others within seven seconds of meeting them."

You may not like or even agree with these bits of advice. But a pastor will ignore them only at risk to his or her vocational future in ministry.

There is a general notion that a pastor should consult with leadership members in the congregation about whether it is time to move on. Sometimes good insight and understanding may result from that. But looking for wise counsel too close within the congregation is not always helpful and may be either self-serving or not reflect the will of the whole.

Pastors who are clear and intentional in their decisions regarding their own vocational future will most often make transitions that are the least confusing to congregations and to their own families. Such important decisions must be made in the context of mutuality for couples and within the overarching framework of discernment and prayer.

Perhaps Moore's most important question is: What are churches looking for? He answers wisely: "Churches are looking for a variety of qualities in their spiritual leader, but they certainly would include most of the following:

- Energy and enthusiasm;
- Faith and spiritual depth;
- Proven qualities of leadership;
- Effectiveness in preaching;
- Pastoral empathy and administrative competence;
- Ability to minister to all members;
- Willingness to commit to the congregation's goals for the future; and
- Proven record of effectiveness in ministry."

July 3, 1997

90. How Newcomers Learn the Rules

There is no place where all these rules are written down; we just know them because that's how we do it.

It's really too early in the morning to be thinking about ministry. But sometimes you just can't help yourself, even on the tennis court.

We play at 6:30 a.m. on Tuesdays and Thursdays. It's a rather motley group of tennis players, most of us in our late 50s and 60s. Two unspoken rules govern our play: play hard to win, and enjoy the game.

We function with more assumptions. Whoever comes plays. That holds true even if we have an odd number. We play two against one; to make it fair the two defend the doubles court and the one defends the singles court. Every game we rotate and the single person always serves.

There is no place where all these rules are written down; we just know them because that's how we do it.

This morning we had a person join us who is new, having only played with us several times in the past. Observing how he functioned within this culture proved fascinating and prompted me to think about pastors who come into congregations as newcomers.

In every group there are two sets of rules. One is official and probably somewhere in print. With tennis, most players know these rules, either from long experience or from watching the game on TV. These are the rules that govern the game.

But the second set of rules is more difficult to learn. It includes understandings, assumptions, "the way we do things around here." They are not written down. They are seldom taught. New people have to learn them just by playing the game and immersing themselves in the culture.

The cultural assumptions on the tennis court were not evident when the ball was in play; then we simply played by the official rules. But how we handled the tennis balls between volleys had to do with the rules of our culture. Do we play with two or three balls? How do you return balls to the person serving so as to minimize the effort to retrieve them? And so on.

The newcomer is at a distinct disadvantage regarding the cultural rules that affect how players interact. Nobody tells the newcomer these unspoken assumptions. Inevitably there are awkward moments and even more awkward feelings. It is easy to understand how newcomers might ask themselves: "Will I ever become a part of the group?"

New pastors coming into a congregation must learn to play by the rules. To learn the first set of rules, they can read the constitution and the bylaws about how things are structured and who has what responsibility. It's more difficult to learn the second set of rules—the culture of the congregation.

Go easy on new pastors. Give them time. Let them learn by observation and by doing. Instead of being critical, why not be helpful and explain the cultural assumptions? To do that, of course, you have to be a thoughtful observer yourself.

What applies to pastors who are new to congregations applies also to all newcomers. And it is why new people need others to build bridges of understanding and relationship. Otherwise they will always feel like outsiders.

Learning the rules when the ball is not in play is essential to feeling acceptance and full participation. Blessed are those congregations that are good teachers in helping pastors and others to play by both sets of rules.

July 17, 1997

91. Evaluate, but Then Look Forward

We need evaluation, but too often we wallow in the mire of everything that is wrong, and that's as far as we get.

Self-assessment is popular and can be useful. From time to time, people and organizations should stop to ask: Who are we? How are we doing? What are we doing?

Recently I was asked how congregations do self-assessments, seeking to grow in self-understanding and to improve the quality of life and ministry. This question came to me in the following form: Is there anything available for congregational evaluation?

My response began negatively. No, we don't have anything for congregational evaluations. Evaluations are looking for trouble, asking about what's wrong. Evaluations are looking at the past.

I wish congregations could turn their eyes toward the future. They need to work from the angle of vision and hope. They need to think positively about goals and growth. Rather than working at evaluations, they ought to set goals.

I am not so naive that I think that we don't need any evaluation. But too often that is where we get stuck. We wallow in the mire of everything that is wrong. And that's as far as we get. Some people seem to even enjoy that process!

And when it comes to congregations, every congregational evaluation ends up in some form of pastoral evaluation. It may not have been intended that way, but that's where it ends. Just ask any pastor.

Having said all that, there are several key issues and questions which might form the basis for a congregational self-assessment. I would ask three questions:

1. What is the emotional and spiritual sense of the congregational self? Congregations have personalities, just as people do.

Is the congregation's identity clear? Does it know who it is and to whom it belongs? How strong is the connection to the larger church? What is the level of self-esteem? Does the congregation have a healthy sense of pride, or does shame better describe the collective self-understanding?

What is the nature of the relationships among members? Do mutuality and togetherness dominate, or do jealousy and antagonism prevail?

2. How well are the systems functioning? A congregation's structure is usually described in its constitution and bylaws, but it can also exist in the unspoken and unwritten consensus of "how things are done around here." How well is that working?

Here one needs to look at structures and issues of governance. Issues of power and who has it—and who feels as though they don't have it—are critical. How are leaders chosen? How are important decisions made? Is there a responsible way to work at good financial management that is forthright, generous, and accountable?

3. Is the program meeting the needs and expectations of the congregation? Every congregation has a certain set of activities—usually under the headings of worship, education, fellowship, and mission—related to the range of ages in the congregation. What are the strengths and weaknesses? In terms of time, energy, and resources, what are realistic goals for program growth? What things have grown old and should be discarded?

A harder question than any of the above is: How do you answer all these questions? Would a congregational evaluation do it? Are pastors, congregational leaders, and even members too close to the situation to perceive it accurately? Does it take a perceptive person from outside the congregation to assist in such a process? Who might that be?

August 21, 1997

201

92. Polarities to Manage in Ministry

Sometimes the question is not how to solve a problem but how to manage polarities.

Should a pastor focus more on being a servant or on being a leader? Do you expect your pastor to focus her or his ministry to you as an individual member with your personal needs or to the congregation as a whole?

Should a pastor give more attention to doing or to being, to the responsibilities of a pastor or to the nurturing of one's own mind, soul, and spirit?

Behind each of these questions is another question: Are these problems to be solved or are they polarities to be managed? That's the question that Barry Johnson would have us ask in his book: *Polarity Management: Identifying and Managing Unsolvable Problems.*

If we assume that these are problems to be solved, then we will try to answer one way or the other: the pastor should focus on being a servant, or the pastor should focus on being a leader. One or the other is perceived to be the right answer to the question.

Polarity management would suggest another alternative. These are not questions to be answered one way or the other. In fact both answers are correct. Good pastors will be both servants and leaders.

Rather than a problem to be solved, the question suggests a polarity to be managed. Sometimes it is important to emphasize being a servant. At other times it is essential to emphasize being a leader. These are polarities that call for wise and good management.

After reading this book several years ago, I asked myself how many polarities like these I could identify that were intrinsic to competent and wise pastoral leadership. Without trying very hard I came up with a list of 33 polarities that pastors need to manage if their ministry is to be effective and fruitful.

Take the second question of the opening paragraph. One aspect of competent pastoral ministry today is ministry to the needs of persons. Pastors minister to persons not only in counseling and visitation, but also by focusing their preaching in a way that is spiritually nourishing to each and every member.

But that is not enough to be a well-rounded pastor today. You are also responsible for managing the congregational system and how the whole functions together for the welfare of the church. Being an effective leader for the congregation as a whole is also a spiritual issue.

To ask whether your concern should be for the individual or for the congregation is to ask the wrong question. It is not a problem to solve but a polarity to manage well as you move back and forth or even weave the two together.

The third question of this column asked about whether the pastor should work more at "doing" or "being." In pastoral circles these days there is a great deal of emphasis on the importance of "being." Who we are is more important than what we do! It is an issue of spirituality.

If the pastor does not nourish the inner self spiritually and intellectually, he or she will have little to offer to others. Thus the emphasis on working intentionally at the one side of this polarity—being.

I have known some pastors, on the other hand, who seem to specialize in going to workshops, accountability groups, and retreats of all kinds, and everything else that takes them away from actually doing anything within their congregation. They can provide a long list of continuing education activities for the year; but you are left wondering if the work of ministry ever gets done.

Competent pastoral ministry is perceived by our ability to manage the polarity symbolized in the words *being* and *doing*.

Now you know three of the 33 ministry polarities that I identified. What similar polarities do you work at managing well? How many similar polarities could you list?

October 2, 1997

93. What's Wrong with "Leadership"?

"Leadership" draws its primary meaning from a secular context and is not adequate to the spiritual dimensions of ministry.

For the last ten years I have been waging a rather quiet campaign not to refer to pastoral ministry by the single word "leadership." The time has come to explain why I believe that this is an inadequate word and why we need to stop using it in this way.

But first let me put in a good word for leadership. Pastors are or ought to be leaders. I don't think anyone believes that more than I do.

One part of pastoral ministry which needs to be reclaimed is our responsibility to be leaders with authority and responsibility within and for the church. The church yearns for pastors with vision and courage.

That is not to say that we want a return to authoritarian leadership—nothing of the sort. Authoritarianism is not acceptable. It never has been. No one has ever wisely chosen persons for leadership who are or were authoritarian in spirit. Authoritarianism is not leadership, but its opposite.

It is ironic that in the very same era that we have almost intentionally taken away from pastors the office of ministry, which involved a clear leadership role, we have resorted to designate pastors under a euphemism by referring to them collectively as "leadership."

Why is "leadership" an inadequate term for pastoral ministry?

1. Leadership describes only one of many pastoral responsibilities. While we rightfully expect pastors to be leaders, that is not all we expect of them. They are also teachers, preachers, and

administrators. They are also counselors, shepherds of the flock of God, and spiritual and pastoral caregivers. They do many things, not all of which can rightly come under the label "leadership."

2. While it is a good and important word, "leadership" draws its primary meanings from a secular context, and therefore is not fully adequate to the spiritual dimensions of ministry. We have appropriately resisted the "chief executive officer" language of the business community when talking about pastors. But by allowing "leadership" to define pastoral ministry we have brought the concept in the back door.

I prefer words that grow out of a service or servant understanding. We need something which reflects a greater appreciation of the relational dimensions of pastoral ministry. We need terms which cause us to be conscious of the spiritual nature of the task. We need a language and an image that is rich in meaning and rooted in Christian tradition.

3. "Leadership" accentuates a functionalist approach to ministry. We too easily fall into notions of ministry as a series of things to do. Now make no mistake about it; there are things that pastors must do. Pastors should have job descriptions which identify tasks and expectations.

But if we have learned nothing else in recent times, we should have learned that ministry has as much to do with "being" as with "doing." Ministry at its best and most meaningful grows out of the persons we are, and are becoming by God's grace.

Ministry has its heart in the sharing of the self. Pastors can do all sorts of things, including the things which leaders must do, but without the joining of soul and spirit, we will miss the heart of the matter.

So what do I propose we use in place of "leadership?" I could be satisfied with several words or combinations of terms. "Ministry" says it all for me, but I know others would like to use that word more broadly to define the responsibility of all Christians.

So maybe we could compromise and use both words: "ministerial leadership." Or "pastoral ministry." Or "pastoral leadership."

The problem with the word "pastor" is that it too easily slips into the framework of one who pastors a congregation. We have others who serve in ministerial leadership roles such as chaplains and missionaries.

Any term that we choose must be adequate to include the whole, and to do so with a richness and breadth that is rooted in all a minister is and does.

December 4, 1997

94. Those Behind the Scenes: Thanks!

Let's not forget the importance of the everyday work of those who serve in essential but often unrecognized ways.

This week I want to give recognition to a group of people who quietly go about their important work, often without expressions of appreciation. Without them, our congregational life together would not be the same.

I write of those special committees who commit their time and energy to serving on special occasions; most often these occasions are weddings, funerals, and anniversaries. Sometimes they are congregational events of celebration or even the Sunday morning coffee time.

This past Saturday my wife and I were asked to serve as ushers for a memorial service in our congregation, a small task we were honored to do in recognition of a member of our Sunday school class.

We were asked to do two things: usher people in for the memorial service and then assist those who stayed for a noon lunch to find their way to tables in the fellowship hall.

Anyone who has ever helped plan a funeral meal understands the difficulty of knowing how many to anticipate serving. It is customary to make a reasonable estimate and then add for a few extras just in case more come than anticipated.

On this occasion, the latter occurred. Tables had been set and food prepared for 120. But people kept coming. We set up an extra table, and that quickly filled up.

Bernice and I had anticipated joining the family and congregation after we had seen to it that all the guests had been seated. But all the seats were taken when the last people had come.

That meant we could eat in the kitchen with the serving committee. Well actually, Bernice and I ate before them, as they brought food back from the tables. I'm glad this happened, since it gave us an insight into the experience from the perspective of the kitchen and the serving committee.

First, it was far from clear that there would be sufficient food, since the number being served was more than expected. I learned that for the serving committee it is often feast or famine.

Well, not exactly famine. But I learned there have been times when there really is no food left for the serving committee.

One server reported the expression of appreciation for using china plates, by now a fairly unusual practice in a throwaway age. But then I learned the dishwasher was not working properly.

Who takes care of such things in a church? And would this serving committee need to wash all these dishes by hand?

By now the line of mostly empty Jell-O bowls was accumulating on the counter. And there were a few sandwiches left as plates came in. The guests had eaten the chocolate cake, of which there had been an abundance; there was an assortment of other flavors left. Yes, we would have plenty, and so would the serving committee.

When we think about our experience of church, we reflect on the big and public events of worship and celebration. These are good and important. But let's not forget the importance of the everyday work of those who serve in essential but often unrecognized ways.

It is in the dozens of dishes of Jell-O salad and the multiple pans of cake that are prepared by members of our congregations. It is in the unheralded but dedicated hours of work put in by serving committees who minister to families and guests setting up and waiting on tables, washing dishes and cleaning up, and eating what remains as their only reward.

Pastors and others would do well to speak a word of gratitude from time to time to those who enable our life together to be what it is by their acts of service and their dedication to the honored ministry of waiting on tables.

January 15, 1998

95. Paradox of Power and Authority

Authority is never clear, never perfect, and never to be fully trusted.

What have we learned about authority and power in ministerial leadership? It seems to me that we should approach this as a paradox. Good leadership thrives on embodying paradox.

The following points summarize how I am working to understand power and authority in ministry.

1. The use of power is not evil. It is intrinsic to life. To be powerless is to be nothing. But many of us function from a stance of perceived powerlessness. Sometimes it seems that way for the church in general.

Ultimately, it does not work that way. Leadership without authority is ineffective. Leadership that is authoritarian is equally ineffective. We are going to have to find some kind of authority between these two extremes.

2. Authority and power in person and office are interrelated and interdependent, and always to be understood together. Authority is given and earned—given in the office and earned in the person.

There is an interesting twist to this in the Greek New Testament words that are often translated as "power" and "authority." The first of these is *dunamis,* from which the word "dynamite" is derived. It has to do with strength, force, and the capability to act. Most of the time it is translated as "power." Power is the ability to act.

The second word is *exousia.* Generally, though not always, it is translated as "authority." This is a derived or conferred authority exercised by virtue of a position or office. When it was said of Jesus that "he taught as one with authority," this is the word used. Authority is the right to act. Both are good words, essential to good leadership and good ministry.

3. Authority is both from above —given by God; and from below—given by the people being served. Both are essential to effective ministry.

Integrated authority has to do with sharing power, such as between a pastor and a congregation. This is collaboration. We want it. We believe in it. But we don't often know how to bring it into being in authentic and life-giving ways. This calls for a lot more thought and work.

4. Authority and power need checks and balances so that they are not abused. We call this "accountability." The primary location for accountability is in the relationships growing out of the office of ministry.

Authority in the hands of those who have no doubts or uncertainty about its use is the most frightening, especially if divine blessing is claimed for it.

Authority is never clear, never perfect, and never to be fully trusted. People with authority should accept the legitimate place of the skeptic, the doubter, the one who questions authority. Skeptics may cause trouble for leaders, but they do everyone a service by helping to keep leaders honest. They are part of the checks and balances that should be in place wherever authority is exercised.

5. Where there is power, there will be resistance. This is predictable, natural, and even desirable, though not always welcome. To exercise power as a pastor is to accept this risk and to make oneself vulnerable to the challenges of others.

Knowing the limits of one's authority is as important as claiming it in the first place. Authority is like emergency power. You're best off when you use it with great discretion and only when it's really necessary.

6. God does not expect or want us to play "spiritual superman." Omnipotence belongs only to God, though the evidence shows God seldom uses it. We could learn from God.

Leaders are also called to be servants—who, by definition,

are without authority and have little power. Paradoxically, there is power in that. The paradoxes of faith never end nor cease to amaze.

February 5, 1998

96. Interviewers Read Between the Lines

The interviewer listens with another set of ears—not to exact words but for insights and perceptions.

I am always on the lookout for opportunities to learn something new that relates to my job. So when a friend and colleague started talking about job interviews, I was all ears. I did my own share of interviewing potential pastors. But almost more than that I saw my task as helping others to conduct interviews with pastoral candidates in helpful and creative ways.

My friend was informally reporting on the research which he and his wife were doing regarding teacher interviews. I saw an immediate connection to pastoral interviews.

The theory goes something like this. In a typical interview the interviewer asks the candidate a series of questions. Typically the candidate assumes that those are the important questions and tries hard to answer them. The interviewer listens to the candidates responses and may even interact with the candidate about them. But, at the same time, the interviewer is listening with another set of ears — not to the exact words but for insights and perceptions about the candidate.

The real judgments about the suitability of the candidate come not directly from the questions and answers but from this finely-tuned skill of listening for the things that really matter.

So as I listened to my friend, I recognized that this is something I have done for years without understanding or knowing how or why I was doing it. It was an intuitive process for which I was now receiving an explanation.

What should one listen for in candidate interviews?

1. Watch for attitudes. Will the person flow toward what is positive and hopeful, or will he or she be quick to join the ranks of the critical and cynical?

2. Does the person accept responsibility for what happens, or does he or she tend to make excuses or blame others?

3. Are there hints of industriousness? A desire to do well? A willingness to initiate ideas and actions? A readiness to go the second mile when duty calls? An awareness that leadership also includes sacrifice?

4. How will the person be perceived by others in this very public role? Is there a willingness to lead as well as a capacity to lead? What is their public persona?

5. Is there any evidence of experienced grace? This is not a belief in God's grace, which ought to be a Christian norm. But has grace, both from God and from others, touched them and made them whole?

6. What is the level of accurate perception? About themselves? About how others see them? About how they see others? How well do they listen?

7. Doing well is not just about working hard; it also has to do with genuine competence to do things right and efficiently. Do you hear hints of genuine competence?

8. Does this person give energy to others in relationships or does he or she consume the energy of others for their personal needs?

This is not a comprehensive list of qualities desired in pastors. But it does illustrate the types of things to listen for in pastoral interviews. Above all, listen with both sets of ears.

If your responsibility for job interviews is with people other than pastors, you might ask whether this system works in other vocations, as well. My guess is that it is universal.

February 19, 1998

97. Avoid the Problems of Nepotism

The problem may simply be in the perception of others. But we should avoid even the appearance of the misuse of family connections.

Life is amazing in its complexity and in our ability to make it complex. Most of the time people bring the best of their intentions to our life together in the church. What we sometimes lack is the best of our wisdom.

The issue for this column is one that few people stop to consider. But in that very lack of thought there is the potential of doing things that result in ill will and conflict.

The word used in political circles is "nepotism." It has to do with favoritism shown to members of one's family, particularly in appointment to political office because of the family relationships. It is viewed as an abuse of power, with the potential of the family system improperly gaining access to roles and relationships that are too close and too private.

Interestingly, my dictionary suggests that nepotism had its origins not in politics, but in the church. The word originated through bishops and church leaders appointing "nephews" to positions of churchly office. Only later was it applied to politics and business.

Does nepotism still occur in the church? Forms of it often occur in small congregations where certain families dominate and control the entire church process. When that happens, one can almost assuredly predict a system that is less than healthy, even though the family will believe it is giving sacrificially to provide leadership in the congregation when no one else will.

Are there other forms of nepotism in the church? If a child of the congregation is hired for some role in the church, should a member of the family be in a position to make decisions related to salary or other terms of the relationship? Probably not.

Spouses of pastors face critical choices that border on this question. Today we encourage pastoral spouses to be members of the congregation like everyone else. That means they should be able to serve in any position for which they have interests and gifts.

Or does it? Any position that deals with issues affecting the pastor is probably inappropriate for a pastor's family member. This makes it very unlikely that a pastor's spouse should serve on a church council or board.

Also, any position that might appear to be an extension of the pastor's influence and power may be suspect if the pastor's spouse assumes a key role within it. So it is not as simple to "be a member like anyone else" as we may have thought.

Another variation on this theme has to do with more than one family member serving on a church leadership group. Is it needed or appropriate for both spouses within one family to serve on the board of deacons or elders? I have seen it happen, even in larger congregations.

To raise questions about spouses serving together assumes that they will always think alike or that they will only represent one perspective. That is not necessarily true. In fact, they may bring more collective wisdom to the church board than any other two people. But does that justify the power that exists within one family when it occurs?

The question is not easily answered. Nor do I necessarily think it should be answered always in one way. But we do need to be alert to the potential of nepotism in the church. The problem may simply be in the perception of others. But since perceptions form reality, we would all do well to take precaution and avoid even the appearance of the misuse of family connections.

March 19, 1998

98. Good Office Secretary Invaluable

It takes an incredible amount of forethought and organization to carry out this complex job.

When a congregation grows to a size or level of activity that requires getting help for the pastor, generally the first thought is to hire an office secretary. Often this begins as a part-time position, sometimes simply as a volunteer to type the weekly bulletin.

In larger congregations, the workload may require more than one full-time professional secretary or administrative assistant. In either case, pastors will attest to the valuable addition such a person brings to the ministry team.

Secretaries do more than type bulletins and letters. Today they must be computer literate and able to manage many types of information.

Most office secretaries assume the receptionist's role. They are the public face for the church five days a week, with a friendly greeting over the phone and a welcoming smile to those who enter the church office, regardless of how busy they are or what deadlines may be pressing. They are on the front lines of hospitality.

No relationship is more important to the functioning of the pastor than the working relationship with the office secretary. If conflict between the secretary and the pastor persists and is not dealt with effectively, it is almost certain the pastor will seek other employment. Underlying this relationship must be respect and loyalty.

That does not mean that there should never be challenge or confrontation to the relationship. A well-organized office secretary has saved the day many times for pastors whose patterns are less disciplined but well intentioned. I can attest to that.

It is inevitable and necessary that the office secretary will be exposed to privileged information. That calls for a high level of knowing when and what information to share.

But even more important, it means knowing and being absolutely trustworthy with information that needs to be confidential. Above all, it means never using the office as a source of gossip, either about pastors or about any of the members.

I have recently been in contact with a congregation that has been working on a job description for the church office secretary. Their good work became the source of inspiration to do this column.

The larger areas of responsibility they described are: receptionist, office management, office administration, secretarial and computer work, and a group of items under "as needed."

All job descriptions need to be understood as describing broad areas of responsibility beyond which there are undefined but reasonable expectations. "Servant leader" describes the role of the office secretary as much as it does the pastor.

The larger the congregation, the more significant becomes the coordinating role of the church office. Maintaining an up-to-date master calendar of events, activities, and room assignments becomes one of the secretary's many important tasks.

Then there are weekly tasks such as the church bulletin and visitor follow-up. There are monthly responsibilities such as a monthly newsletter. And some major jobs are done annually: compiling the yearbook, collecting reports for business meetings, and working with denominational and conference questionnaires.

It takes an incredible amount of forethought and organization to carry out this complex job.

One question that often comes up is whether the office secretary should have to type all the minutes of all the committees and boards. In our congregation we have tried to avoid that by requesting that committee and board secretaries submit copy ready materials. The pastor would do well to help protect the secretary from an overwhelming workload.

A highly competent church office secretary who brings strong relational skills and a clear sense of Christian service is a person to be valued and affirmed. Speak a word of gratitude to that person the next time you have opportunity to do so.

April 2, 1998

99. Parable of Rabbit, Cat, and Fence

Who are we keeping in? Who are we keeping out? What are we protecting by our fences? How high must our fences be?

It's been a dreary spring in Kansas. Yesterday we had more drizzle, and it was far too cold for this time of the year when one's thoughts turn to the out-of-doors.

But today the sun is mostly shining and the wind is moderately blowing. The wheat and the grass are fully green; the redbuds are about to bloom. Nature holds promise.

For some, spring means the return of baseball and the hopes of a winning season for a favorite team. For others, spring brings the return of hope that this year the garden will produce as bountiful a crop as the garden catalogs of January always promise. We're more of the latter sort.

Some people seem to think Bernice and I are avid gardeners. We don't quite think of ourselves in that way. But we do raise some vegetables. Our ever bearing raspberries have been improving. We continue to work at roses and perennials.

Mostly we enjoy the work. It's good therapy. And we take pride in eating off of the land in our small corner of the earth.

Gardening in Kansas is always a challenge. With summers that are far too hot for many living things, one has to depend on early spring for the cool season crops.

So, on the one reasonable though cool evening this week, Bernice persuaded me that it was time to put up the rabbit fence. That is the 18-inch chicken wire fence designed to keep the rabbits out. In it we grow lettuce, green beans, spinach, and kohlrabi—things the rabbits love to consume along with our tulip leaves. Rabbits run fast, but rabbits don't jump—not even 18 inches.

Cats, by comparison, are slow. But they can jump. Our 14-year old cat, Tippy, routinely explores his world around the garden, inside and outside the fence. Tippy and the rabbits live more or less at peace with each other—co-existence, one might call it. Both have learned what they can and can't do, so Tippy long ago gave up chasing rabbits.

But never underestimate the power of temptation. Last spring we woke up one morning to discover a rabbit inside the fence feasting on the tender new growth of things rabbits love. He was trapped by temptation.

What to do? Have you ever tried to catch a rabbit that can't jump the fence? Well, that didn't work. Aha! Call the cat. So we did. And now Tippy was inside the fence—with the rabbit. But not for long! Cats are powerful motivators in confined spaces. The rabbit got out—and never got inside the fence again.

There must be a parable in that experience. It set me to musing about fences and gardens and rabbits—and cats. What are fences for? Keeping things in or keeping things out? Who are we keeping in? Who are we keeping out? What are we protecting by our fences? How high must our fences be? Do we need to build our fences higher since they were breached once?

Robert Frost wrote: "Good fences make good neighbors." But for rabbits and cats it didn't work out that way. And we like our neighborhood and our neighbors—without fences.

Cats and rabbits can live at peace outside the fence. But inside the fence together—well, that's another story. I assume both cats and rabbits live according to their natural instincts—doing what nature has programmed into them. Most of the time that serves them well. But sometimes it doesn't.

If we're thinking about congregations, who are the rabbits and who are the cats? How are they living together? What role do fences play in our relationships?

We put up the same fence again this year, still expecting to keep the rabbits out. But I wonder about the church.

April 16, 1998

100. Belief, Unbelief Both Take Faith

The point of faith, it seems to me, is that there is always some uncertainty, some risk, some doubt.

It takes as much faith not to believe in God as it does to believe in God.

This is not a carefully reasoned theology. Nor am I about to make a rational case for why the existence of God should be obvious for any thinking person. That's been tried and proven unsatisfactory.

Some ministers give the impression that belief in God is easy and is to be expected of anyone with a religious inclination. I do not count myself among them. To believe in what is not obvious to our senses or our experience is not easy.

The point of faith, it seems to me, is that there is always some uncertainty, some risk, some doubt. Faith without doubt is not really faith at all, but credulity— the tendency to believe something too easily. There is no virtue in being gullible, especially about things religious. The world has too much of that kind of religion already.

Often people think faith is only necessary if one believes in God. This leads to the conclusion that not to believe in God is to operate on the side of certainty. People assume atheists don't need faith.

That isn't how I see it. To me, faith is part of the bargain either way. In both cases, there is some uncertainty, some risk that what you give yourself to may prove untrue, unreliable or inadequate.

Similarly, the assumption is often made that to believe in God is to close off options, that it forces one into a kind of dishonesty and denial of reality. Along with that is a popular secular assumption that not believing in God opens options that narrow-minded believers cannot experience.

I don't get it. For me, belief in God opens possibilities to a universe still developing. It is atheism that chooses to close at least one way of understanding life and space. Maybe it's a matter of perspective or an inclination to believe the worst about each other. We all tend to define more narrowly that which we choose not to believe.

To believe in God is to indulge in an adventure. It is like traveling into new lands and territories. It is to journey with Abraham. It is to explore the unknown. I have always been more impressed by the hiddenness of God than by God's self-disclosure. We have only hints of God's being, reflections in a mirror. Nothing is really all that obvious. It certainly was not with the incarnation of Jesus. You had to believe to get it. And even then, those closest to him had their doubts.

Nevertheless, the life of faith and belief has its attractions. To cast one's lot with belief is to live on the shore of affirming life. To believe is to say that doubt and skepticism, while never far away, have their limits. Life will be lived on the positive rather than on the negative, with what you believe rather than with what you disbelieve.

With all the attendant risks, believing gives me joy.

August 6, 1998